Scarf designed by Jan Mayer   Photographed by Ralph Gabriner   Model Laura Caulfield

THE COMPLETE
BOOK OF SCARVES

D1534409

Scarf designed by Cynthia Wayne Gaffield   Model Ryanne Webster

THE COMPLETE BOOK
OF SCARVES

all you need to make,
decorate, embellish, tie & wear

jo packham

STERLING PUBLISHING CO., INC. NEW YORK
A STERLING/CHAPELLE BOOK

Scarf designed by Roberta Glidden   Model Ryanne Webster

Library of Congress Cataloging-in-Publication Data

Packham, Jo
    The complete book of scarves : all you need to make, decorate, embellish, tie & wear / by Jo Packham.
        p.   cm.
    "A Sterling/Chapelle book."
    Includes index.
    ISBN 0-8069-0428-3
    1. Scarves. 2. Textile painting. 3. Fancy work. I. Title.
    TT667.5.P33 1998   97-35570
    646.4'8–dc21   CIP

A Sterling/Chapelle Book

10 9 8 7 6 5 4 3 2 1

First paperback edition published in 1999 by
Sterling Publishing Company, Inc.
387 Park Avenue South, New York, N.Y. 10016
© 1998 by Chapelle Limited
Distributed in Canada by Sterling Publishing
% Canadian Manda Group, One Atlantic Avenue, Suite 105
Toronto, Ontario, Canada M6K 3E7
Distributed in Great Britain and Europe by Cassell PLC
Wellington House, 125 Strand, London WC2R 0BB, England
Distributed in Australia by Capricorn Link (Australia) Pty Ltd.
P.O. Box 6651, Baulkham Hills, Business Centre, NSW 2153,
Australia
Printed and bound in China
All rights reserved

Sterling ISBN 0-8069-0428-3 Trade
              0-8069-7781-7 Paper

for chapelle, ltd.

owner
jo packham

editor
malissa moody boatwright

staff
marie barber, ann bear, areta bingham, kass burchett, rebecca christensen, holly fuller, marilyn goff, shirley heslop, holly hollingsworth, shawn hsu, susan jorgensen, leslie liechty, pauline locke, ginger mikkelsen, barbara milburn, linda orton, karmen quinney, leslie ridenour, and cindy stoeckl

photographer
kevin dilley/hazen photography

photography styling
jo packham

designers
robin bergman, joanna chrysohoidis, michael davis, cynthia elmore, james elmer, carol freeman, cynthia wayne gaffield, roberta glidden, mary jo hiney, gail mackenzie, jan mayer, yoriko nishi, joy peterson-anckner, jamie pierce, vickie hu poirier, rhonda rainey, sarah mays-salin, paula chaffee scardamalia, barbara conover scoville, penny toliver, nancy welch, pamela whitlock, and rebekah younger

If you have any questions or comments or would like information on specialty products featured in this book, please contact: Chapelle, ltd. ▪ P.O. box 9252 ▪ Ogden, UT 84409 (801) 621-2777 ▪ Fax (801) 621-2788

Due to the limited amount of space available, we must print our patterns at a reduced size in order to give our patrons the maximum number of patterns possible in our publications. We believe the quality and quantity of our patterns will compensate for any inconvenience this may cause.

The written instructions, photographs, designs, patterns, and projects in this volume are intended for the personal use of the reader and may be reproduced for that purpose only. Any other use, especially commercial use, is forbidden under law without the written permission of the copyright holder.

Every effort has been made to ensure that all the information in this book is accurate. However, due to differing conditions, tools, and individual skills, the publisher cannot be responsible for any injuries, losses, and other damages which may result from the use of the information in this book.

Scarf designed by Yoriko Nishi

Laurel Birch once said, "I live within the vivid color of my imagination . . . ." and I believe that to be true of most artists and most frustrated souls who so want to be artists. I know because I am one of those souls. One of those who is unable to express with my own hands the world of art and design that can so vividly be seen in the unrestricted boundaries of my imagination.

To express what I can so vividly see, therefore, I have surrounded myself with those who are unquestionably the elite of those talented and respected personalities in design, art, and handcrafted work.

When the decision was made to compile a book on designing, wearing, and decorating with scarves, I had the opportunity to again enlarge my own confines of creativity and imagination to include the fashionable world of wearable art designers. Their technical skills as well as their sense of color and execution of design are to be not only admired but envied and desired.

The artists with whom we work to create such enchanting alluring pieces, whether they be the scarves on the following pages or the finest wood boxes found in other publications, often times design pieces that are irresistible. When this occurs it is not enough for me to simply include them in our publications. The longing to own them is unyielding and inevitable.

My home and life are consequently filled with the beautiful objects that friends and associates have created. I try to find ways to enhance every corner of my life with them. For example, I just recently used hand-dyed scarves by Roberta Glidden to cover a dark window whose view was much obstructed. Now the not so desirable view is one of soft colors and fine silk and one I look forward to admiring in the light of dawn or the darkness of night.

As I grow, so grows my passion for art and with its use or its purchase, each piece of art has its greatest purpose fulfilled. May you always be surrounded by the beautiful and the artful.

Jo Packham

contents

Model Ryanne Webster

general instructions

introduction to making scarves

Signature artists from across the United States have combined with talented Chapelle artists to present a collection that is a bold exploration of design techniques for making, decorating, and embellishing scarves.

These techniques include weaving, knitting, dyeing, stenciling, painting, rubber stamping, beading, accenting with ribbon embroidery, creating with machine embroidery, and applying unusual edge treatments.

In-depth instructions are provided for creating scarves from scratch—in all shapes and sizes. There are also quick and easy ideas for embellishing and personalizing a purchased scarf—making it one of a kind.

A special section of the book is dedicated to the art of tying and wearing these original hand-made or embellished scarves.

It is also appropriate to display these works of art in the home. Use the ideas featured in the decorating with scarves section and discover how these rich textures can inspire family and friends to express themselves in like fashion.

how to make a basic scarf

Scarves may be made in any size. Basic square scarves range in size from 30" to 45". Large square scarves worn as shawls, range from 54" to 60". Rectangular scarves range in width from 4" to 11" and range 45" to 72" in length.

Make a scarf that is in proportion to one's body size. Measure a favorite scarf to determine the size that is most flattering.

When making a scarf, cut the fabric on the grain line. Pull the crosswise and lengthwise threads at the desired measurements and cut along the pulled threads.

fabric selection for scarves

The most important consideration in selecting fabric for a scarf is that it be drapable. Soft, silky fabrics drape well and tie easily. For casual scarves, use fabrics such as lightweight cottons, and rayon crinkle. For dressier scarves use fabrics such as silk charmeuse, chiffon, or velvet.

Remember, purchasing fabric is not always necessary. Huck toweling, an old table cloth, or discarded curtains may be used as scarf fabric.

materials used in scarf design techniques

acid dyes:
Acid dyes are concentrated, powdered, hot water dyes that produce the most vibrant results on protein fibers including silk, wool, cashmere, nylon, and feathers. Acid dyes are used to paint and dye fabric.

color & dye remover:
This mixture may be used to create designs or correct mistakes by removing unwanted dye. Read and follow manufacturer's instructions. Use in a well ventilated area.

embossing powders:
Embossing powders are available in many colors. These powders are poured over pigment inks. Excess should be shaken off, and powder set by using a heat tool.

Note: Clear embossing powder will stay on fabric longer than metallic embossing powder.

fabric dyes:
Fabric dyes penetrate fabric fibers with a soft feel. Fabric dyes may be used on any fabric, including silk. Thin fabric dyes with water for watercolor effects.

fabric inks for stamping:
Textile inks are specially formulated for use with fabrics. They are permanent and washable. They are available in a sponge top bottle or may be spread onto an un-inked stamp pad. Read and follow manufacturer's instructions.

fabric paints:
Fabric paints are used to outline or accent painted designs. They dry soft to the touch. Fabric paints may be thinned with water for watercolor effects. *Note: It is important that fabric paints be "flowable" watery paints. Some fabric paints are thick and are unsuitable for certain dyeing projects.*

gutta resist:
Gutta resist is used to draw borders of an image on silk, stopping the flow of dye at the resist lines. Resist should be completely dry before applying dye. Gutta resist is available in clear, black, gold, and silver. Clear resist may be removed by dry cleaning but colored resist should not be dry cleaned.

plastic squeeze applicator:
Plastic bottles may be used for applying resist or fabric paints. They are available in fine to ultra-fine tip for better detail during application.

rubber stamps:
Rubber stamps come in many shapes and sizes. They are inexpensive, versatile implements for making projects more colorful and personal.

stabilizers:
Stabilizers should be used to prevent puckering and distortion of fabric. Stabilizers may be used when fabric cannot be drawn upon. Tissue paper may also be used as a stabilizer. Water-soluble stabilizer washes out easily. Heat sensitive stabilizer is removed by a hot iron when work is completed.

stamp pads:
Use a colored stamp pad or blank stamp pad and bottled ink applied to stamp pad.

stem bamboo brushes:
Stem bamboo brushes are specifically made to use with ink, dyes, and watercolors. They are available in 3-stem and 4-stem.

water-soluble resist:
Water-soluble resist is used to draw borders of an image on silk, stopping the flow of dye at the resist lines. *Note: Line is not as reliable as when using gutta resist.* Water-soluble resist washes out easily with warm water, even after steaming.

transferring patterns on scarves

graphite paper:
Graphite paper is coated on one side. When it is pressed by a pencil, it transfers the graphite or chalk to the surface under it. Use paper made especially for fabrics.

tracing paper:
Tracing paper is thin enough to see through and allows original pattern lines to be retraced easily.

water-soluble stabilizer paper:
Stabilizer paper is used when fabric cannot be drawn upon. Trace design onto a sheet of water-soluble stabilizer using a white marker. Trim away excess stabilizer.

Pin traced design onto right side of fabric or embroidery area. Stitch design directly through stabilizer. Trim excess stabilizer. To remove stabilizer, touch sheet with moistened cotton ball to dissolve.

There are two methods for transferring patterns. Choose the method that is most comfortable and convenient. If directions indicate enlarging pattern, place pattern in a photocopy machine. Set the machine to percentage required and enlarge.

method one (graphite paper) instructions:

1. The photocopy of pattern may be traced onto tracing paper and transferred onto the item using graphite paper.

2. Position carefully and tape graphite paper between pattern and item with graphite side facing item. Firmly trace the pattern using a pencil or stylus. Lift corner slightly and make certain the pattern is transferring.

method two (template) instructions:

1. The photocopy of pattern may be traced onto and cut from a manila envelope or mylar, making a template.

2. Position carefully and tape template on item. Carefully trace around template using a subtle color of chalk.

3. Remove the template once the design has been transferred.

how to care for scarves

It is advisable not to wash scarves very often. Spot cleaning is best when needed. Be certain to read and follow manufacturer's washing and handling instructions for fabric, materials, and accessories or embellishments with each scarf. Otherwise, use the following as general guidelines:

acrylic scarves:

Hand wash. Lay flat to dry. Iron on low setting using a dry iron.

dyed scarves:

Dry clean or hand wash in cold water using a gentle soap or shampoo. Hang to drip dry. Iron on low setting.

scarves with embossing powders, stamping ink, or stenciling paint or dyes:

Spot cleaning is recommended. However, they may be dry cleaned or hand washed. Do not dry in dryer or apply any heat such as ironing. Some inks will wash out if not heat set.

polyester scarves:

Hand or machine wash in cool water, gentle cycle. Hang to drip dry. Iron on low setting.

scarves with silk ribbon embellishing:

Machine wash in cold water using mild detergent on delicate cycle, or hand wash in cold water using mild detergent. Iron background fabric only.

silk scarves:

Dry clean. Solid colors may be hand washed in cool water using mild detergent. Hang to drip dry. Iron on low setting.

wool scarves:

Dry clean or hand wash in cool water, roll in dry towel to remove excess water. Lay flat to dry. Iron on low setting.

edging techniques for scarves

hemming scarves

machine-stitched narrow hem:

1. Machine-stitch ¼" from fabric edges, using coordinating lightweight thread. Fold one edge to wrong side on stitching line. Press fold.

2. Stitch close to fold, using short stitch length. Trim excess fabric close to stitching.

3. Fold folded edge to wrong side. Stitch even distance from edge. Repeat for remaining edges.

hand-stitched narrow rolled hem:

1. Thread needle with one strand of coordinating lightweight thread. Knot end. Position needle at edge of fabric and roll fabric ¼" around needle. Remove needle.

2. Insert needle under the roll and out through top of roll. Stitch, holding fabric taut. Keep needle at 45°. Space stitches ⅛" apart.

3. Continue rolling edge of fabric with fingers and stitching roll in place. Thread should encircle roll on wrong side.

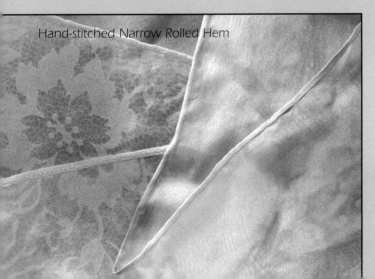

Hand-stitched Narrow Rolled Hem

scalloped edge scarf

designed by Chapelle
See photo on page 15.

materials:

scarf fabric: desired size (model was made with huck toweling)
tea bags (8)
thread: coordinating

implements:

iron and ironing board
needle: hand-sewing
pan to tea dye
scissors: fabric
sewing machine
straight pins

instructions:

1. Using fabric scissors, cut two pieces of scarf fabric desired size.

2. Remaining fabric was tea dyed for scallops. To tea dye, place eight tea bags into pan filled with water. Heat over medium temperature until mixture is hot, but not boiling. Immerse fabric in mixture to soak for at least 30 minutes. When fabric has been dyed to desired color, remove from pan and wring out. If possible, hang fabric outside to dry (to make dye darker).

3. Refer to **scallop pattern** on page 12. Using fabric for scallops, transfer pattern onto fabric for each edge of scarf. See **diagram 1** on page 12. Position line of circles so there is ½" gap at each open end, ⅝" gap in between each circle, and 1" gap between bottom of each circle and raw edge.

4. Machine-stitch along line of scallops and cut out. See **diagram 2** on page 12.

5. Trim edges to ¼" and cut between scallops. See **diagram 3**. Turn right side out. Press. Place one piece of scarf fabric on working surface. Place desired number of scalloped edges along each edge of scarf fabric, lining up raw edges, leaving ½" gap at each end. See **diagram 4**. Pin, baste, and machine-stitch down each side.

6. Place remaining piece of scarf fabric over first piece. See **diagram 5**. Pin, baste, and machine-stitch front to back using ½" seam, leaving one end open to turn. Be careful to stitch just inside seam attaching scallops to front piece.

7. Turn scarf right side out. Press. Hand-stitch opening closed.

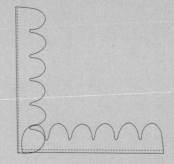

diagram 4

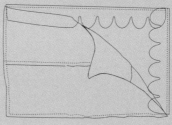

diagram 5

scallop pattern
enlarge 145%

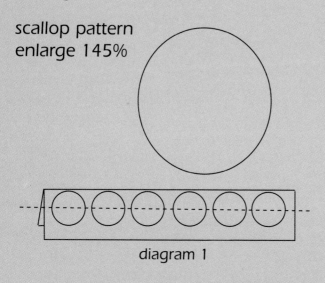

diagram 1

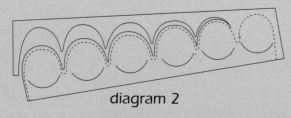

diagram 2

diagram 3

blanket stitch edge scarf

designed by Chapelle
See photo on page 15.

materials:
scarf fabric: desired size (model was made with table cloth)
thread: pearl cotton #5, coordinating

implements:
needle: chenille, size 20
scissors: fabric
sewing machine

instructions:
1. Using fabric scissors, cut two equal pieces of scarf fabric along desired pattern on fabric in desired width and length.

2. With right sides together, machine-stitch ¼" seam along all fabric edges, leaving an opening for turning. Turn right side out.

3. Whip-stitch opening closed. Using needle and pearl cotton #5 coordinating thread, blanket-stitch along all fabric edges.

blanket stitch:

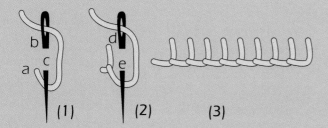

(1) (2) (3)

1. Bring needle up at a, down at b. Bring needle up again at c, keeping thread under needle.

2. For second stitch, go down at d and back up at e. Continue in same manner.

3. Completed blanket stitch.

box pleated edge scarf

designed by Chapelle
See photo on page 15.

materials:
scarf fabric: desired size (model was made
    with print curtain for scarf and solid and
    print curtain fabric for pleats)
thread: coordinating

implements:
iron and ironing board
scissors: fabric
sewing machine
straight pins

instructions:
Note: If scarf fabric is 3 yds., use 1½ yds. solid pleat fabric and 1½ yds. print fabric.

1. Using fabric scissors, cut print and solid fabric into strips 1½ times longer than they are wide. Machine-stitch strips together alternately with right sides together to form a long strip. Press seams. When desired length, sew short ends together.

2. Press seams open. With wrong sides together, fold completed circle in half lengthwise. Press fold line.

3. Fold fabric 1" onto itself on both sides. See **diagram 1**. *Note: If using striped fabric keep pattern same on each boxed section.* Pin pleat in place on raw edge. Repeat all way around strip. Baste-stitch pleats in place. Press. Lay border out with even number of pleats along edges of scarf fabric. See **diagram 2**.

4. Cut into raw edges of fabric as far as seam allowance on corner pleats. See **diagram 3**. Lay front panel right side up. Place border over it with large box pleats facing down. Match corners and line up raw edges. Pin and baste-stitch border to front panel, taking ½" seam.

5. Place back panel over bordered front piece, right sides down, and line up the four sides. See **diagram 4**. Pin and baste-stitch around three sides, leaving one end open to turn. Turn right side out. Slip-stitch opening closed on back side.

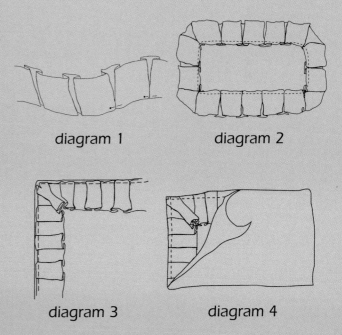

diagram 1 diagram 2

diagram 3 diagram 4

13

bow tie edge scarf

designed by Chapelle
See photo on page 15.

materials:

ribbon: desired variety, ½ yd. per bow
scarf fabric: desired size (model was made
  with toweling)
thread: coordinating

implements:

iron and ironing board
needle: hand-sewing
scissors: fabric
sewing machine

instructions:

1. Using fabric scissors, cut two pieces of scarf
fabric desired size. With right sides together,
machine-stitch two pieces of scarf fabric
together along two long sides and one short
end. Turn scarf right side out. Press seam to the
inside on open short end. Hand-stitch opening
closed.

2. Cut ribbon into 18" lengths. Hand-stitch
ribbons on each short end of scarf. Tie ribbons
into bows.

crochet edge scarf

designed by Chapelle
See photo on pages 15 and 16.

materials:

scarf fabric: 9½"-wide unfinished or 8½"-wide
  finished, 82" long, to accommodate
  crochet edge
thread: mercerized crochet cotton

implements:

crochet hook: size 10
iron and ironing board
scissors: fabric
straight pins

abbreviations:

ch	chain stitch
dc	double crochet
sl st	slip stitch
sc	single crochet
sk	skip
sp	space
st(s)	stitch(es)
hdc	half double crochet
lp st	loop stitch
p	picot
p-loop	picot-loop
*	Indicates work following the * is to be repeated number of times indicated.
( )	Indicates what is enclosed in the ( ) is to be repeated number of times indicated.

instructions:

<u>Row 1:</u> Join to one corner, *ch 7, p, ch 9, p,
ch 3, sc in next 4th sp, (ch 7, p, ch 9, p, ch 3,
sc in next 5th sp) 5 times, p-loop, sc in block
corner, (p-loop, sc in next 10th ch st) 7 times to
corner of next block. Repeat from * around,
with an extra p-loop at each corner. Fasten off.

<u>Row 2:</u> Join to a corner loop, (p-loop, sc in
next loop) around with an extra p-loop at each
corner. Fasten off.

<u>Row 3:</u> Join to one corner, *ch 7, p, ch 16, dc
in 8th st from hook, ch 3, sk next 3 sts, sc in
next 4 sts, ch 6, p, ch 3, sc in next loop. Repeat
from * around, with 2 extra loops at each
corner. Fasten off.

<u>Row 4:</u> Join to one loop, ch 3, (4 dc, 4 ch, p,
and 5 dc) in same loop, * ch 1, (5 dc, p, and 5
dc) in next loop. Repeat from * around. Join
and fasten off. Stretch and pin right side down.
Steam and press dry through a cloth.

Crocheted lace trim should measure
approximately 8½". Hand-stitch trim to each end
of finished scarf, making certain crocheted
eyelet side is up. Gently press scarf and lace.

Left to right: Bow tie Edge Scarf, Box Pleated Edge Scarf, Blanket Stitch Edge Scarf, Scalloped Edge Scarf, and Crochet Edge Scarf

Left to right: Crochet Edge Scarf and
Cotton Fringe Edge Scarf

cotton fringe edge scarf

designed by Chapelle
See photo on page 16.

materials:
fringe: cotton twisted, ecru, 26"
scarf fabric: desired size
thread: coordinating

implements:
iron and ironing board
ruler or tape measure
scissors: fabric
sewing machine
straight pins

instructions:
1. Using fabric scissors, cut off fabric selvages. Cut two pieces desired scarf size. Place and pin fringe across edge of fabric. Machine-stitch in place with ½" seam allowance. Repeat on other fabric edge.

2. With right sides together, pin both pieces of fabric together with fringe to inside. Machine-stitch around fabric edges, leaving 3" open to turn fabric. Trim fringe in seam allowance to ¼". Zigzag-stitch through all thicknesses to prevent fraying of fringe

3. Turn scarf right side out. Slip-stitch opening closed. Zigzag-stitch across fringe along seam to prevent fraying of fringe. Press scarf.

balled edge scarf

designed by Chapelle
See photo on page 18.

materials:
fiber fill: polyester
scarf fabric: desired size for scarf front, back, edges, and balled edges
thread: coordinating

implements:
iron and ironing board
needle: hand-sewing
scissors: fabric
sewing machine
straight pins

instructions:
1. Using fabric scissors, cut one piece of scarf fabric desired size. Cut one piece of contrasting fabric same size for scarf backing. Cut two pieces of contrasting fabric 1½"-wide by scarf length for long edges. Cut two pieces of contrasting fabric 1½"-wide by length for short edges. With right sides together, machine-stitch scarf front and backing fabric together, taking ¼" seams up long sides. Leave short ends open. Turn fabric right side out.

2. Press long edges of backing fabric in ¼" on each side. Using sewing machine, top-stitch long edges of backing fabric to front of scarf up long sides.

3. Measure short edges of scarf to determine number of balled edges required. Space balls 2" apart. Using remaining contrasting fabric, cut desired number of 3½"-diameter circles. Place fiber fill in center of circle. Using hand-sewing needle and coordinating thread, gather around edge of circle. Wrap thread around forming a stem. Repeat for required number of balls.

4. Fold short edges of scarf in ¼" and pin balls between front and back of scarf. Using one contrasting piece of fabric cut for short edges, press one edge under ¼". Place and pin edge fabric to scarf, turning short end in ¼". Top-stitch through all layers. Repeat on remaining short end of scarf.

Model Ryanne Webster

Balled Edge Scarf

18

ethnic edge scarf

designed by Joy Peterson-Anckner
See photo on pages 6–7.

materials:

beads: glass pony (96); odd-shaped (72)
cording: satin, 3⅜ yds.
fiber fill: polyester
floss: pearl cotton, 4 yds.
fray preventative
fringe: knotted; braid; brush; loop
scarf fabric: desired size; coordinating colors
   for balled edges (4)
thread: coordinating for hemming scarf;
   coordinating pearl cotton for balled edges

implements:

needles: hand-sewing; tapestry, size #18
scissors: fabric
sewing machine

instructions:

1. Using fabric scissors, cut two pieces of scarf fabric desired size. With right sides together, machine-stitch two pieces together taking ¼" seam, leaving short ends open.

2. To make balled edges, cut desired number from coordinating fabric 1" x 2½", alternating colors. Machine-stitch three edges, taking ¼" seams, forming a tube.

3. Stuff open end of tube with fiber fill. Wrap open end tightly with pearl cotton. Place ball edges on both edges of scarf ½" apart. Measure and cut knotted fringe into four 14" lengths. Apply fray preventative liberally at cut marks. Let fray preventative dry. Cut fringe desired length. Hand-stitch one length each to bottom front and bottom back of scarf fabric. Repeat on other scarf end.

4. Measure and cut braid into four 14" lengths. Apply fray preventative liberally at cut marks. Let fray preventative dry. Trim braid if needed. Hand-stitch one length of braid on top of knotted fringe edge on front. Hand-stitch second length of braid 2" above first braid. Repeat on other scarf end.

5. Measure and cut cording into two 48" lengths. Apply fray preventative. Pinch and twist ends until fray preventative dries or holds form. Working with one length, fold one end 2" back on itself and tie a top knot. Cut off tail and apply fray preventative. String five pony beads onto cording. Tie knot tightly at bottom of last bead. Cut off tail and apply fray preventative. Repeat process until both 48" lengths of cording are used. Makes 12 beaded tassels.

6. Apply fray preventative to tops of 12 remaining knotted tassel fringe. When completely dry, cut knotted tassels, flush with knot, from connecting braid. Hand-stitch one knotted tassel to bottom knot of each beaded tassel.

7. Evenly space six beaded tassels along bottom front edge of scarf. Hand-stitch corded knot on top of braid. Repeat on other scarf end.

8. Measure and cut brush fringe and loop fringe at 1" intervals. Apply fray preventative liberally at cut marks all the way through the connecting braid. Let fray preventative dry. Set aside.

9. Measure and cut cording into four 40" lengths. Apply fray preventative. Pinch and twist ends until fray preventative dries or holds form. Working with one length, fold one end 2" back on itself and tie a top knot. String one copper bead, two pony beads, and one copper bead onto cording.

10. Using one 1" length of fringe (brush or loop) and hand-sewing needle and thread, tack left edge to cording. Roll fringe piece around cording and tack closed. Using tapestry needle with six strands of floss, bring floss up through bottom of tassel. Wrap floss twice around base

of tassel head, through head body, then wrap top part of tassel head twice. Knot floss and run tail through body. Push fringe back and clip both floss and cording. Repeat for all tassels. Makes 10 brush fringe tassels and eight loop fringe tassels.

11. Evenly space tassels on both ends of scarf along top lengths of braid. Hand-stitch into place.

Ethnic Edge Scarf close-up

rouched edge scarf

designed by Chapelle

materials:
cording
scarf fabric: desired size for scarf; lining, same
    size as scarf fabric; lightweight for edging
thread: coordinating

implements:
iron and ironing board
needle: hand-sewing
scissors: fabric
sewing machine
straight pins

instructions:

Note: Edging fabric needs to be 2½ times length of cording. Using fabric scissors, cut edging fabric to fit loosely around cording, allowing a ⅜" edge. Wrap and gather-stitch fabric around cording. Gather fabric on cording.

1. Pin edging to wrong side of scarf fabric, facing inward, adjusting gathers at corners. Baste-stitch together.

2. Cut and pin lining fabric to scarf fabric with edging. Machine-stitch together through all layers, leaving an opening to turn scarf. Turn scarf right side out.

3. Using iron and ironing board, press scarf. Stitch opening closed.

Rouched Edge Scarf

Scarf designed by Nancy Welch   Model Ryanne Webster

Fringe Tassel Edge Scarf

fringe tassel edge scarf

designed by Nancy Welch
See photo on page 21.

materials:

fringe: upholstery, ½ yd.
scarf: long or square
thread: coordinating

implements:

needle: hand-sewing
ruler or tape measure
scissors: fabric
sewing machine

instructions:

1. Using fabric scissors, cut fringe into two equal pieces for each end of scarf.

2. Thread needle. Using hands, gather one short end of scarf. Tightly and neatly wrap banded edge of one piece of fringe just above one end of scarf edge. See **diagram 1**. Turn under and cut end of fringe. Hand-stitch in place, stitching through to scarf so tassel and scarf are securely attached. Repeat on other scarf end.

3. See **diagram 2** for completed tassel. Tassel was embellished with rows of seed beads stitched over fringe edge and swags of seed beads draped from top or embellish as desired.

Refer to Nancy Welch's publications, *Tassels*, and *Tassels, the Fanciful Embellishment* for other tassel variations and ideas.

diagram 1   diagram 2

It was quite by accident that **Nancy Welch** found herself a foremost authority on tassels. With a Master's Degree in art and teaching textiles in the California college system she assigned tassels as an art project in 1977. The work her students turned in was so impressive - one student braided her children's hair to form a tassel while another unravelled a thrift store sweater - that she decided to research tassels.

What she found was that no one else had done any documentation on them, despite the fact that they have been in continual use since before recorded history and appear in all cultures that she studied. "I have dated them from 7000 B.C.", she says. "No form of ornament has been as widely used for as many years as the tassel. Yet they serve no function other than decoration. They decorate for kings and commoners, in palaces and yurts, on priceless jewelry, and on work animals. Perhaps they are the thread that binds us all together." Her enthusiasm has led her to write *Tassels*, and *Tassels, the Fanciful Embellishment*. Her third book is awaiting publication.

beading edges on scarves

needles & thread:

When beading on very soft, fine fabrics, a regular beading needle and fine silk thread or cotton embroidery floss are good choices. Separate the plies of cotton and use only one ply at a time. A #9 embroidery needle is ideal when working with seed beads size 11/0 or larger.

Choose a neutral color thread that is similar in theme to your bead design. It is nearly impossible to string beads without a little thread showing between the beads. Light nylon may be used where strength is a consideration. Metallic threads are not recommended because the surface fiber tends to fray and ravel.

stringing beads:

Work with thread doubled to make two strands. Use double knots to begin and end strands. Slip one bead over needle and position it about 3" from long end of thread. Loop the thread back through the bead and pull it tightly. The purpose of this "stopper" bead is to keep the design pattern beads from slipping off the needle. Secure stopper bead to a flat surface to stabilize thread.

Thread beads of row from top to bottom. See **diagram 1**. The needle should emerge from top bead. Double knot to end string.

surface beading:

Surface beading requires beads to be sewn on individually and may be done on any material through which a beading needle may pass. The method used to make the stitch is largely determined by the type of bead being sewn.

For small areas and tight curves, it is best to sew on each bead individually. Bring needle up from back to front through beading surface in desired location. Slip bead over needle and guide it all the way down the thread until it rests on beading surface in desired place. Bring needle back through beading surface into the same hole or very close by so the bead is secured to surface. See **diagram 2**.

The shape of the bead determines which method of sewing will be best. If a bead is donut-shaped, it will probably be best sewn using the technique shown in **diagram 3**. Long narrow beads may be treated in a similar manner to bugle beads shown in **diagram 4**. Faceted or large round beads may be sewn on as shown in **diagram 5**.

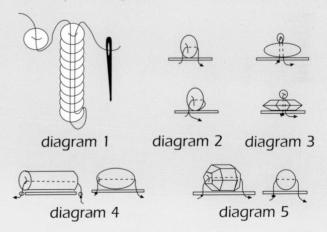

diagram 1   diagram 2   diagram 3

diagram 4   diagram 5

Rose Beaded Edge Scarf

rose beaded edge scarf

designed by Chapelle

materials:

beads: #3 bugles, purple and dk. blue rainbow, (1 hank each); 12/0 seed, gray (1 hank); pearl (1 strand); 11/0 seed, purple transparent (2 hanks); blue rainbow (2 strands); green transparent (1 strand); blue-green transparent (1 strand); yellow transparent (1 hank); red rainbow (1 hank)

scarf fabric: width of beaded trim

thread: beading, size a & d

implements:

beeswax or paraffin

marker: fine-point

needle: beading, size 13

paper

instructions:

Hint: Use a fine-point marker to mark off pattern every 10 beads. This forms a grid that makes the pattern easier to read.

1. Draw a 3" line on piece of sturdy paper. Measure each fringe before turning to make certain each one is even. Refer to rose fringe pattern on page 24 to work project.

2. Soak beading thread in water to remove sizing. This will cut back on tangling. Run thread over piece of beeswax or paraffin while working. This will protect thread from cutting on glass beads.

3. Top of fringe is 83 beads long and seven rows wide in size 12/0 seed beads. Fringe is 3" long in size 11/0 seed beads.

top of fringe:

Row 1: all 12/0 gray seed beads.

Row 2: two 12/0 gray seed beads, one pearl 12/0 seed bead through entire row.

Row 3: all 12/0 gray seed beads.

Row 4: all #3 bugle beads.

Row 5: all 12/0 gray seed beads.

Row 6: two 12/0 gray seed beads, one pearl 12/0 seed bead through entire row.

Row 7: all 12/0 gray seed beads.

4. Using size a beading thread, thread one gray bead, one bugle bead, and one gray bead. Thread another gray bead, one bugle bead, and one gray bead. Insert needle through first gray bead, bugle bead, and gray bead. Beads will now be lined up side by side. See **diagram 1** on page 26.

5. Thread back through second gray bead, bugle bead, and gray bead. Continue for 83 rows. See **diagram 2** on page 26. The strip will be approximately 6" long. Tie off and thread ends through bugle beads.

6. Connect thread to 6" strip at one end threading it through the end of gray bead on first row. This will start second row of gray beads and pearl beads. Thread two gray beads. Go back through second gray bead on first row of gray beads on the strip. Bring needle up through third gray bead. Thread on another gray bead, go back through second gray bead. Come back up through third bead and thread on pearl bead. Go back through previous bead to second row of gray beads and come up through pearl bead. Repeat pattern of two gray beads and one pearl bead to end of row.

7. For third row, repeat second row using all gray beads. At end of row, thread needle through end of beads to the opposite end of the strip. Turn strip over and repeat three rows of beads on other side. Tie off thread. See **diagram 3** on page 26.

8. For fringe, using size d beading thread, attach thread to the strip and sew in the end. Thread on 3" of purple beads. Use last bead as a turn bead, thread back through beads and into first gray bead on fringe. Thread needle back through second gray bead on first row of strip to begin second fringe. Thread on 3" more of purple beads. Repeat for eight fringes of purple beads.

9. For first bead of rose, placement is important. Because bead sizes vary, establish center bead on 3" strip. The center bead row in rose fringe pattern below is marked. Thread on purple beads to 1½". Add 11 to 12 more beads. Thread red bead, continue with purple to end of 3". Thread needle back through fringe and into strip. Begin next fringe as before. Continue until first rose is finished. Thread on all seven purple fringes. Turn strip over and work pattern backwards to repeat second rose. Following second rose will be eight purple fringes.

rose fringe pattern

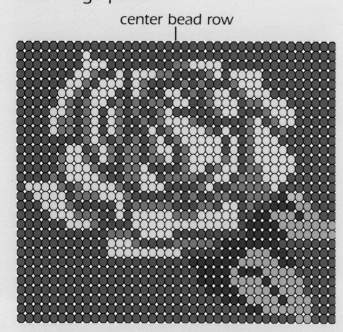

center bead row

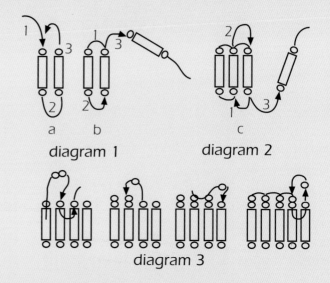

diagram 1   diagram 2

diagram 3

beaded edge scarf

designed by Chapelle
See photo on page 28.

materials:

beads: 11/0 seed, purple (1-2 pkgs.)
scarf fabric: desired size
thread: coordinating; waxed cotton-wrapped
  polyester for beading

implements:

needle: beading
scissors: fabric
sewing machine

instructions:

1. Machine-stitch ¼" from raw edge of scarf fabric. Fold raw edge along stitching line and fold over one more time. Machine-stitch narrow hem along scarf edges.

2. Thread beading needle with single strand of cotton-wrapped polyester thread. Bring needle up at edge of fabric and through three seed beads. Take short stitch in edge of fabric so third bead lies next to first bead and second bead is raised away from fabric. Take next stitch close to previous stitch. Continue beading all edges of fabric.

dangle beaded edge scarf

designed by Chapelle

materials:

beads: 11/0 seed, transparent crystal
    (2 pkgs.); 6mm round, frosted amber
    (214); faceted bright green (48); faceted
    gold (48); fancy shaped flower head (10);
    38mm antique bugle, amber (36)
scarf fabric: desired size
thread: fine silk, coordinating

implements:

iron and ironing board
needles: beading; hand-sewing
ruler or tape measure
scissors: fabric
sewing machine
straight pins

instructions:

1. Cut one piece of scarf fabric desired size
for scarf. Hand-stitch narrow rolled hem
along scarf edges.

2. Refer to photo below. Add dangle beading
to both ends of scarf.

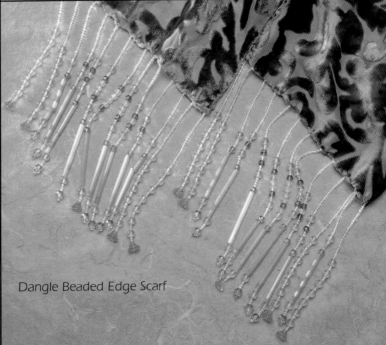

Dangle Beaded Edge Scarf

Model Kamden Quimbey

Barbara Conover Scoville lives in South Jordan, Utah where she teaches and designs handknit silk beaded purses. The owner of a small business called The Heirloom Knitter, she is dedicated to reviving old arts, and creating gifts of the hand and heart. A knitter for the past 20 years, Barbara is inspired by the legacy of handwork left by those of yesteryear and is dedicated to keeping their memory alive.

knitted & beaded edge scarf

designed by Barbara Conover Scoville

materials:

beads: 11/0 seed, blue iris (5 hanks)
scarf fabric: double width of knitted beaded
   edge (appropriate for long rectangle scarf)
threads: silk, black, size e (1 spool);
   coordinating

implements:

cookie sheet
iron and ironing board
nail polish: clear
needles: double point, size 0000 (2);
   embroidery for tying loose ends; hand-sewing
scissors: fabric
sewing machine
ruler or tape measure

Left to right: Beaded Edge Scarf and Knitted & Beaded Edge Scarf

Barbara Conover Scoville

abbreviations:

K   knit

B   bead

SB   Insert needle as if to knit. Before completing stitch, slip up required number of beads. The number after the SB designates how many beads to slip up. The beads will rest between the stitches after the next stitch is knit. *Note: All beads are placed on wrong side of work but will show up on right side of work.*

*   *   repeat within the asterisk

instructions:

Refer to **general instructions** on pages 8–10.

1. It is helpful to transfer beads on left side of cookie sheet and the silk on right side of cookie sheet.

2. Using fabric scissors, cut one end of a strand of beads from the hank. Remove enough beads (about 2") to tie a loose single knot. Slip end of thread through loose knot and tighten knot.

3. Slide beads horizontally over knot onto thread. If a bead will not pass over thread, simply untie, remove bead, re-tie, and begin the process again. After all beads from the strand have been transferred, cut strand from hank.

4. Transfer a total of six strands of beads onto thread, sliding beads far enough down thread to have some working thread.

5. When close to using all beads strung, finish the row, leaving a 6" tail and cut thread. Transfer six more strands of beads and continue tying new end in.

6. Using long tail cast on method, cast on 72 stitches.

Row 1-4: knit.

Row 5: K4, *SB1, K1* (65 times) end K3.

Row 6: knit.

Rows 7, 9, 11, 13, 15, 17, 19, 21, 23, 25, 27, 29: repeat row 5.

Rows 8, 10, 12, 14, 16, 18, 20, 22, 24, 26, 28, 30: repeat row 6.

Row 31: K4, *SB 50, K1* (65 times), end K3. *Note: This is the fringe row. Ten strands of beads transferred onto silk are needed to complete this row. After completing the fringe row, transfer another six strands of beads to finish scarf edge.*

Row 32: knit.

Rows 33, 35, 37, 39, 41, 43, 45, 47, 49, 51, 53, 55, 57: repeat row 5.

Rows 34, 36, 38, 40, 42, 44, 46, 48, 50, 52, 54, 56, 58: knit.

Rows 59-61: knit.

7. Cast off loosely. On wrong side of scarf edging, tie in loose ends by running ends with embroidery needle through five purl bumps, then knotting them. On wrong side of work, dab very small amount of clear nail polish to seal.

8. Measure width of knitted beaded edge. Double the width, adding ½" to allow ¼" seam allowance. Cut scarf fabric. With right sides together, fold fabric lengthwise. Machine-stitch taking ¼" seam. Leave one end open for turning. Turn and press. Zigzag-stitch opening closed.

9. Hand-stitch knitted beading to each edge using very tiny stitches.

special care:

Hand wash scarf in cold water. Hang to dry. Do not iron beading.

embellishing purchased scarves

sequined scarf

designed by Mary Jo Hiney

materials:

beads: 11/0 seed, frosted yellow-orange
(2 pkgs.); 11/0 seed, lt. mauve (1 pkg.);
11/0 seed, lt. purple-pink rainbow (1 pkg.)
floss: lt. green, 3 yds.
purchased scarf or fabric: 44"-wide voile,
pale yellow, 10" x 44"
sequins: standard, clear iridescent, 2 yds.
silk ribbons: 7mm pale yellow; lt. purple,
2½ yds. each
synthetic ribbon: 4mm lt. green, 3 yds.
thread: coordinating

implements:

iron and ironing board
needles: beading; embroidery, size 9 & 3;
hand-sewing
scissors: fabric
sewing machine
straight pins

instructions:

See **general instructions** on pages 8–10 and
ribbon techniques for scarves on pages 54–55.

1. Machine-stitch narrow hem along all edges
of scarf fabric.

2. Refer to sequined scarf placement diagram.
Slightly fray pale yellow ribbon. Pull a center
fiber from frayed end and gather ribbon. Pin
gathered ribbon onto scarf end, turning ribbon
ends under as needed. Using hand-sewing
needle and coordinating thread, tack ribbon to
scarf. Repeat with lt. purple ribbon at opposite
scarf end.

3. Separate sequins from strand. Using beading
needle, hand-stitch sequins along gathered
pale yellow ribbon ¼" apart. Use yellow-orange
beads to anchor sequins to ribbon. Use lt.
mauve beads to anchor sequins to lt. purple
ribbon.

4. Using three strands of floss and embroidery
needle, stem-stitch stems near gathered lt.
purple ribbon. Slip three lt. mauve beads onto
needle for flowers along stems near pale
yellow gathered ribbon. Use yellow-orange
beads for flowers near lt. purple gathered
ribbon.

5. Press all work as necessary on wrong side of
fabric.

special care:

Hand wash scarf in cold water. Do not press.

sequined scarf placement diagram
enlarge 210%

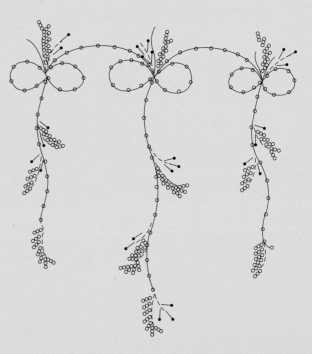

Sequined Scarf

Mary Jo Hiney attributes her creativity to having mastered the basics as a child seamstress. After high school, she attended the Fashion Institute of Design and Merchandising in Los Angeles, California. She got her start in the downtown garment industry before moving to NBC in Burbank, California. Eventually the pace became to restricting, so Mary Jo and her family moved to the beautiful and tranquil central coast of California.

It was here that Mary Jo discovered her creative genius, the love of raising a family, and the joy of life.

It is Mary Jo's hope to inspire others to unleash the "child within" to create their own masterpieces.

Mary Jo Hiney

Photographed by Scott Caraway

machine embroidery technique

Materials used for machine embroidery may be bought from most craft or department stores. Any fabric may be used for machine embroidery. Consider how the texture will affect the finished piece.

materials:
scarf fabric
stabilizer: water-soluble
threads: invisible; machine embroidery; metallic machine embroidery; sewing

implements:
bobbins
cotton ball
marker: white
needles
sewing machine
straight pins

instructions:
1. Stabilizers should be used to prevent puckering and distortion of fabric. Water-soluble stabilizer will stabilize work on sheer fabric. Stabilizer may be used when fabric cannot be drawn upon.

2. Trace design onto a sheet of water-soluble stabilizer using a white marker. Trim away excess stabilizer.

3. Pin traced design onto right side of embroidery area. Stitch ribbon or thread design directly through stabilizer. Trim excess stabilizer.

4. To remove stabilizer touch sheet with moistened cotton ball to dissolve.

butterfly scarf

designed by Vickie Hu Porter
See photo on opposite page.

materials:
embroidery hoops: 5", 8", plastic and metal spring type
purchased scarf or fabric: chiffon, silk, or polyester, 3 yds.
paillette: gold, for eyes, size #14 (1 gm. pkg.)
threads: blending filament, dk. colors, amethyst; confetti blue; confetti green; confetti pink; navy; purple; royal (50mm each)
blending filament, dk. colors:
    black high luster; confetti; confetti fuchsia; peacock (100mm each)
blending filament, lt. colors:
    grapefruit glow in dark; star blue; star pink; star yellow (50mm each)
blending filament, lt. colors:
    starburst; star mauve; pearl (100mm each)
blending filament, accent colors:
    blue; chartreuse; copper; fuchsia high luster; garnet; pink; purple; red; sapphire; turquoise (50mm each)
Japanese gold for veins, edging, and bodies:
    #1 gold, 144 yd. cone (3);
    #4 very fine braid gold, 11M reel (3)
invisible nylon, size #80: clear; smoke, 1500 yd. spool each; coordinating silk or polyester for hemming
stabilizer: water-soluble

implements:
bobbins: (12 or more)
marker: ultra-fine tip, permanent, black
needles: hand-sewing; sewing machine microtex sharp 130/705 h-m, sizes #80/12, #60/8; metalfil 130/705 h-m, size #80
scissors: fabric
sewing machine: zigzag with adjustable tension bobbin case

instructions:

Refer to **general instructions** on pages 8–10.

1. Using fabric scissors, cut fabric 20" x 108". Using hand-sewing needle and coordinating thread, hem all edges of scarf fabric using hand-stitched narrow rolled hem.

2. Refer to butterfly scarf patterns on page 36. *Note: In order to waste less stabilizer, trace butterflies on long lengths of stabilizer.* Using marker, trace butterfly patterns of choice, close together, onto 18" length of stabilizer, leaving 1½" margin around edge of stabilizer. Place traced butterflies on two layers of stabilizer same size. Place the three layers in 8" embroidery hoop with tracing on top.

3. Wind bobbins with an assortment of lt. and dk. blending filaments, accent colors, and nylons three-fourths full.

4. Insert microtex needle, size #60/8, in sewing machine. Lower feed dog. Remove presser foot or use foot for free motion sewing.

5. Use smoke nylon for top and bobbin thread. Set tension on balanced settings. Slide hoop under needle. Lower presser bar. Take one stitch and draw bobbin thread to top. While holding threads, stitch two or three stitches in place. Cut thread ends. *Note: Do this with every thread change.* See **diagram 1** on page 37 to form invisible thread foundation. Outline butterfly wings and body then fill in with a grid pattern ⅟₁₆" apart, catching outline. Fill head and body more closely.

6. Use clear nylon in lt. areas and smoke nylon in dk. areas. *Note: If stabilizer tears, add another piece and keep sewing.*

7. Change bobbin to blending filament. Loosen bobbin tension slightly. In needle, use smoke nylon for dk. filaments and clear nylon for lt. filaments. See **diagrams 2a and 2b** on page 37 for adding color. Fill in wings in circular motion using a short stitch length. Stitching should interlock to form interconnected web. Bobbin thread should barely be seen on top as a color. Parallel straight stitching can also be used as fill for contrasting textures.

8. Fill with lt. and dk. colors in areas indicated on butterfly pattern(s). Overlap stitches slightly where two colors meet. The object is to create a netting with no large holes and gaps. Be certain to catch edges of wings. Check underside of hoop occasionally to catch missed areas.

9. Insert microtex needle, size #80/12, in sewing machine. Fill bobbin with accent color. Tighten top tension one or two steps from normal. Loosen bobbin tension. Zigzag-stitch to fit spots and bars. Change width of stitch to make irregular width shapes while sewing. Bobbin tension should be loose enough to come to the top to create a double-sided effect.

10. Use clear nylon for top thread and Japan very fine #4 braid gold thread in bobbin. Change to straight stitch. Loosen top tension slightly. Loosen bobbin tension to fit braid. Adjust tension as needed so braid stays on bottom and top thread holds it snugly. Begin at butterfly head and outline wings and body. Be certain to catch the edges of the body. Fill body by stitching lines close together. See **diagram 3** on page 37.

11. Use clear nylon for top thread and gold Japan #1 for bobbin thread. Set top tension normal and bobbin tension should be tightened to fit thread. Using narrow 1.5mm zigzag stitch, outline butterfly wings covering gold braid thread. Do not fill in body.

12. Insert metalfil needle, size #80, in sewing machine. Use Japan gold #1 thread for top and bobbin thread. Change to straight stitch. Set tension on balanced setting. If it becomes difficult to keep embroidery in the hoop, dispense with it now. See **diagram 4** on page 37. Straight-stitch veins in one continuous line back tracking when necessary. Each line should have two touching rows of stitching. Be certain to catch the edges of wings.

13. Trim away excess stabilizer leaving ¼" around. Wash butterfly in warm water. Lay flat to dry. Trim any loose threads. If there are any large gaps, place another piece of stabilizer over butterfly and restitch.

14. To attach butterflies to scarf, place and pin onto scarf.

15. Insert microtex needle, size #60/8, in sewing machine. Use smoke nylon for top thread and gold Japan thread for bobbin thread. Set tension on balanced setting. Working on wrong side of scarf and using 5" embroidery hoop, straight-stitch butterfly body to scarf. Begin at top of butterfly head, go around body, and end at top of butterfly head.

16. Make certain scarf fabric is tight in hoop. *Note: For following step, test on scrap piece of fabric before sewing scarf fabric. If fabric puckers use a piece of tissue paper or stabilizer.* Stitch feelers free hand using very small stitch length so fabric will not pucker. Back track the feelers like the veins and finish at butterfly head.

17. Using hand-sewing needle and smoke nylon thread, hand-stitch paillettes on for eyes.

18. To make a folded butterfly, trace a left wing with a body attached and a left wing. Finish to veining, but do not sew gold braid on body.

Cut out the bodiless wing and place it on the wing with a body. Stitch it down where it meets the body, then sew the gold braid on the body.

Note: There are 29 butterflies on model scarf. Materials listed will make approximately 34 butterflies with blending filaments left over. Make as many butterflies as desired. Use all the patterns or one or two. Make them in many colors or use a specific color scheme. The scarf can be used as a table runner or window dressing. Pins, barrettes, Christmas ornaments, and other items can be made using the butterflies. Kreinik threads, blending filaments, and paillettes were used in machine embroidering the butterflies.

special care:

Hand wash scarf. Steam press on polyester setting on wrong side of scarf. To maintain beauty of Japan threads, dry cleaning is recommended.

Butterfly Scarf close-up

butterfly scarf patterns   enlarge 165%

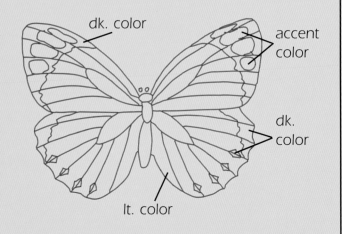

dk. color

accent color

dk. color

lt. color

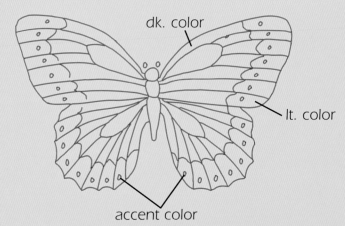

dk. color

lt. color

accent color

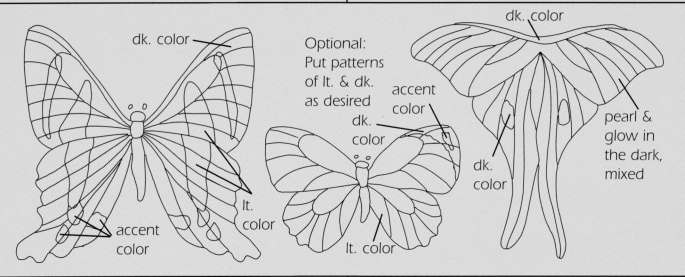

dk. color

lt. color

accent color

Optional:
Put patterns
of lt. & dk.
as desired

accent color

dk. color

lt. color

dk. color

dk. color

dk. color

pearl & glow in the dark, mixed

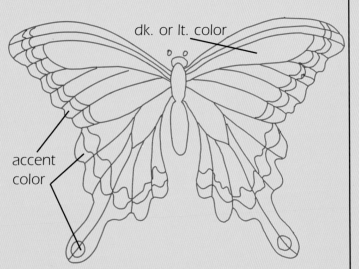

dk. or lt. color

accent color

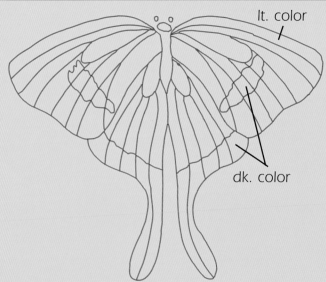

lt. color

dk. color

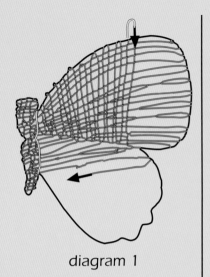

diagram 1

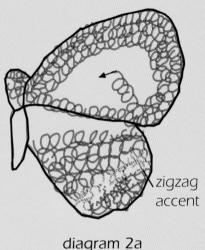

zigzag
accent

diagram 2a

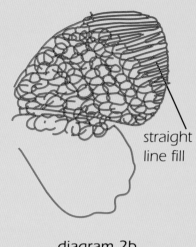

straight
line fill

diagram 2b

diagram 3

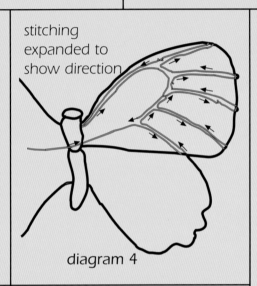

stitching
expanded to
show direction

diagram 4

Vickie Hu Poirier is a textile artist living in New Mexico. She designs and creates wearable art and large scale wall quilts. Vickie loves to use many techniques in her work, but she is best known for her appliqué.

Vickie's work is strongly influenced by her beliefs as a member of the Baha'i Faith. "I see all the races and cultures of the earth as flowers in one garden, the founders of the world's great religions as soaring in the same heaven, deriving their inspiration from the same Divine Source. My art demonstrates this unity in the charming combination of diverse textile elements and cultural influences."

Vickie's work is on permanent exhibit in China, India, the Fiji Islands, and in locations in the United States, including Chicago and the United Nations in New York City. She also designs for Kreinik Manufacturing Company, Inc., who commissioned her to design the beautiful Butterfly Scarf featured in this book.

Kreinik Manufacturing Company, Inc., known as a pioneer for bringing the industry innovative threads, offers the largest selection of soft and easy-to-use metallic and silk threads, plus real metal threads, for all hand and machine embroidery.

37

basket weave scarf

designed by James Elmer

materials:

beads: 8mm bugle, gold (15)
pearls: 5mm (5)
purchased scarf or fabric: silk charmeuse, peacock, ⅓ yd.; brocade, gold metallic, scrap with pattern
sequins: 6mm cup, clear fuschia iridescent (15)
stabilizer: heat sensitive
threads: gold lurex; cotton – black; turquoise; teal; avocado, (1 spool each)

implements:

iron and ironing board
needles: hand-sewing
scissors: fabric
sewing machine: 3-thread embroidery
straight pins

instructions:

1. Attach heat sensitive stabilizer to fabric using straight pins. Simply remove stabilizer with hot iron when work is complete.

2. All work on this project was done free hand. Chain-stitch using black and alternating with teal thread for basket weave pattern. Use turquoise and avocado thread to loosely connect teal and black basket weave. Appliqué floral design using gold metallic brocade fabric in empty space between black and teal basket weave pattern. Cut away excess fabric. Chain-stitch using teal thread to highlight floral pattern and cover appliqué edge. Add gold lurex thread around appliqué to outline.

3. Highlight appliqué using sequins anchored by a bugle bead and place a pearl in center.

4. Remove stabilizer. Sew all sides, leaving an opening to turn fabric. Turn fabric and hand-sew opening closed.

chain stitch:

1. Bring needle up at a. Keep thread flat, untwisted and full. Put needle down through fabric at b and back up at c, keeping thread under needle to form loop. Pull thread through, leaving loop loose and full.

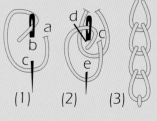

2. To form next chain loop, which holds previous one in place, go down at d and back up at e. Continue to form each chain loop in same manner.

3. Finish with a short straight stitch over bottom of last loop to secure in place for a completed chain stitch.

38

Upon graduation James was not only successful on both the stage and screen, but his embroidery work was in demand as well. He was head of the embroidery department for Eaves-Brooks Costume for several years.

James' small scarves are uniquely designed, versatile, and have multiple uses. His designs have been seen around the world and worn by celebrities from Bette Midler and Pavorotti to members of Ringling Brothers Circus.

James now lives with his cat "Puddie" in the 100-year-old farmhouse built by his grandfather next to the home in which he was raised. James enjoys what he always missed while living in New York City – the majestic beauty of the Wasatch Mountains.

James Elmer was born in Marriott, Utah. He graduated from Weber State University with a double major in art and theater arts.

James has included additional photos of "gallery" scarves that demonstrate what can be accomplished after mastering this technique.

39

jeweled scarf

designed by Chapelle

materials:
purchased scarf or fabric: size, color, and
   pattern desired
rhinestones with nailheads: assorted
studs with nailheads: medium gold

implements:
pliers

instructions:
Refer to **general instructions** on pages 8–10.

1. Using pliers, and following pattern of scarf
fabric, attach studs and rhinestones as desired,
inserting nailheads through right side of scarf.

special care:
Hand wash scarf in cold water. Press as
necessary from the back side of scarf.

oriental appliquéd scarf

designed by Chapelle

materials:
fabric: cream (⅛" yd.); rust (⅛")
floss: rust
purchased scarf or fabric, 45": green (1 yd.)
silk ribbon, ⅛": green (14 yds.)
thread: cream, green, rust

implements:
carbon paper
dressmaker's pen
manila paper
tracing paper

instructions:
Refer to **general instructions** on pages 8–10.

1. If constructing scarf, from green fabric, cut two 17" x 45" pieces.

2. Trace entire enlarged **oriental appliquéd scarf pattern** on page 42 onto one piece of manila paper by placing carbon paper between tracing paper and manila paper. Cut only outside edges of design.

3. Using dressmaker's pen, trace pattern onto each end of right side of one piece of scarf/green fabric with design centered horizontally and 1¾" up from edge of fabric.

4. Cut individual pattern pieces from manila paper.

5. Place vertical line of each pattern piece on grain of right side of fabric. Using dressmaker's pen, alllowing for ¼" seam allowance to be added when cutting, and matching pieces with colors indicated on patterns, trace each pattern piece onto fabric.

6. From cream fabric, cut two of pattern 4; reverse pattern and cut two more. Cut two of

pattern 7; reverse pattern and cut two more.

7. From rust fabric, cut two each of patterns 2, 3, 5, and 6; reverse patterns and cut two more of each. Cut two of pattern 1.

8. Determine which pieces will extend under adjoining pieces. Seam allowances should be turned under only on edges not covered by another appliqué piece. All edges should be turned under on pieces which do not touch others. On curved edges which will be turned under, clip seam allowances. Fold on pencil line and finger press.

9. At one end of scarf, place one piece at a time within outline following the numerical sequence indicated on pattern pieces. Slip-stitch each piece with matching thread along folded edges. Stitches should be placed evenly about

⅛" apart and pulled taut. Inside corners may need additional stitches for reinforcment. For outside corners, stitch up to folded corner, then fold under seam allowance of other side and turn corner with stitching. Repeat appliqué for remaining end of scarf.

10. Using a dressmaker's pen, draw pattern for embroidery in center of flowers. At one end of scarf, and using rust floss, sew **backstitch** for stems and **satin stich** for stem ends. Repeat for flowers on remaining end of scarf. Rinse with water to remove all pen markings. Press from wrong side of fabric.

11. If constructing scarf, place right sides of green fabric pieces together and stitch with ½" seam, leaving 6" opening. Trim corners and turn. Slip-stitch opening closed and press.

12. Cut silk ribbon into fifty 10" lengths. Using green thread, tack centers of 25 lengths to one end seam of scarf at ⅝" intervals. Knot ribbon over tacking. Repeat for remaining end. Knot each end of ribbons.

backstitch:

1. Bring needle up through fabric at a and go down at b, just to the right of a. Bring needle up through fabric at c, to the left of a. Repeat b–c, inserting the needle in the same hole that was a.

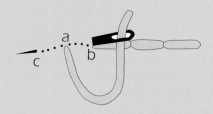

satin stitch:

This stitch may be worked vertically, horizontally, or diagonally. Stitches may be the same length or in graduations.

1. Bring needle up through fabric at a and go down at b, forming a straight stitch. Bring needle up through fabric at c and down again at d, forming another smooth straight stitch that is touching the first.

2. Repeat to fill design area.

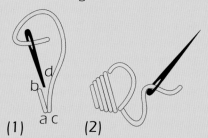

(1)   (2)

oriental appliquéd scarf pattern
enlarge 200%

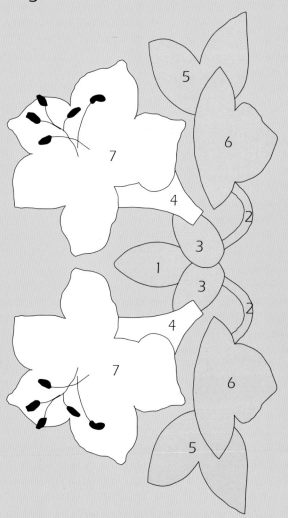

42

photo transfer scarf

designed by Chapelle

materials:
color copy of desired motif
photo transfer medium: clear
purchased scarf or fabric: polyester crepe,
    ivory, 45" x 45"
thread: coordinating

implements:
scissors: craft; fabric
sewing machine
sponge
straight pins

instructions:
Refer to **general instructions** on pages 8–10.

1. Machine-stitch narrow hem along all edges of scarf fabric.

2. Trim around color copy motif.

3. Apply photo transfer medium to color copy. Place color copy face down and centered on one corner of scarf. Let transfer medium dry thoroughly.

4. Using a wet sponge, saturate paper of color copy in a circular motion.

5. Remove all paper from color copy, leaving motif image on scarf.

6. Let scarf dry thoroughly.

special care:
Hand wash scarf in cold water. Do not press.

rubber stamping & stenciling scarves

rubber stamping technique

materials:
acrylic paints
cork adhesive and strips
embossing powder
fabric dye
fabric ink for stamping
fabric paints
frame: stretcher bars, wood strips, or foam
   board (slightly larger than scarf fabric)
paintbrushes: watercolor, sm.; med.; lg.
plastic squeeze applicators
   for resists and fabric paint
resist: gutta; water-soluble
rubber stamps
scarf fabric
stamp pad(s)

implements:
bleach (optional)
embossing heat gun
iron and ironing board
paper
push pins
ruler or tape measure

instructions:
1. When using rubber stamp, cover entire rubber stamp with fabric ink.

2. Rubber stamp techniques used on projects in this book are a combination of rubber stamp, fabric dye, and fabric paint.

3. Lay out desired design on paper to determine placement of rubber stamp designs, resist lines, fabric dye colors, and fabric paint highlights. Keep this pattern near work area for reference.

4. Assemble frame. If using wood, place cork strips around frame using cork adhesive. Stretch fabric across frame and secure with push pins.

5. Follow individual project instructions.

stencil technique

materials:
acrylic paints
scarf fabric
sponges
stencils: pre-cut
textile medium

implements:
masking tape
palette sheet: all-purpose, disposable
paper towels
rubbing alcohol
scrap paper

instructions:
1. This technique is used to force paint through a pre-cut shape. Practice design on scrap paper before beginning project.

2. Hold or tape stencil securely to project. Using paper palette, prepare mixture of each color of acrylic paint and textile medium following manufacturer's instructions.

3. Using sponge, load with small amount of paint. Blot sponge on paper towel until most of the paint has been removed. Apply the paint to project by lightly "blotting" the sponge up and down. Use less paint and apply several coats.

4. Using rubbing alcohol, clean stencils if they are to be used as a reverse design.

Scarf designed by Cynthia Elmore

45

Stamped & Beaded Scarf

stamped & beaded scarf

designed by Cynthia Elmore
See photo on page 45.

materials:

acrylic paints: bronze; copper; gold
beads: coordinating as desired
embossing powders: bronze; copper; gold
fabric paints: dimensional, copper; gold
foam brush
frame: foam board, 40" square
plastic squeeze bottle: ultra-fine tip, 2 oz. (5)
rubber stamps: desired pattern (3)
scarf fabric: 36" square
spray webbing: gold
textile medium
thread: coordinating for hemming; braid

implements:

embossing heat gun
iron and ironing board
masking tape
old newspapers
palette sheet: all-purpose, disposable
paper towels
sewing machine

instructions:

Refer to **general instructions** on pages 8–10.

1. Using masking tape, tape one side of fabric to foam board. Tape opposite side, stretching fabric gently. Make certain fabric is taut.

2. Using old newspaper, practice using spray webbing. Read and follow manufacturer's instructions. Apply spray webbing onto fabric.

3. Allow spray webbing to dry for one hour. Prepare mixture of each color of acrylic paint and textile medium following manufacturer's instructions. Using foam brush, spread thin layer of paint mixture onto palette sheet

keeping colors separate. Press stamp design into paint mixture and stamp onto fabric. Wipe stamps on damp paper towel and repeat process varying colors and stamp designs, overlapping patterns. Apply embossing powders to enhance images. Set powder using a heat tool. Using squeeze bottles, acrylic paint mixture, and fabric paints, outline stamped designs as desired.

4. Remove fabric from foam board. Let paints dry thoroughly. Machine-stitch narrow hem along scarf edges. Embellish scarf with beads and braid as desired.

special care:

Spot clean scarf. Dry clean if necessary.

four women scarf

designed by Cynthia Elmore
See photo on opposite page.

materials:

fabric dyes: dk. blue-green; lt. blue-green; dk. green; purple-blue; yellow-green; golden-yellow; med. yellow-green
fabric paint: gold
frame: stretcher bars or wood strips (slightly larger than fabric)
paintbrushes: watercolor, sm.; med.; lg.
plastic squeeze applicator: fine-point
resist: water-soluble
rubber stamp: four women design
scarf fabric: desired color and type, 18" x 60"
thread: coordinating

implements:

iron and ironing board
push pins
sewing machine
ruler or tape measure

instructions:

Refer to **general instructions** on pages 8–10.

1. Wash fabric. Using iron and ironing board, iron fabric dry. Using rubber stamp design and gold fabric paint, stamp design three times across narrow width at each end of fabric 1¾" from cut edge. Let paint dry thoroughly. Attach fabric to frame using push pins.

2. Apply water-soluble resist. Using paint-brushes and fabric dye, paint colors as desired. Let fabric dry thoroughly. Remove fabric from frame. Heat set color by ironing at temperature setting suited for fabric.

3. Using cool water, wash out resist from fabric. Squeeze out water (do not wring). Iron dry at temperature setting suited for fabric. Machine-stitch narrow hem along scarf edges.

special care:

Hand wash scarf in cool water. Do not wring. Press on cool setting.

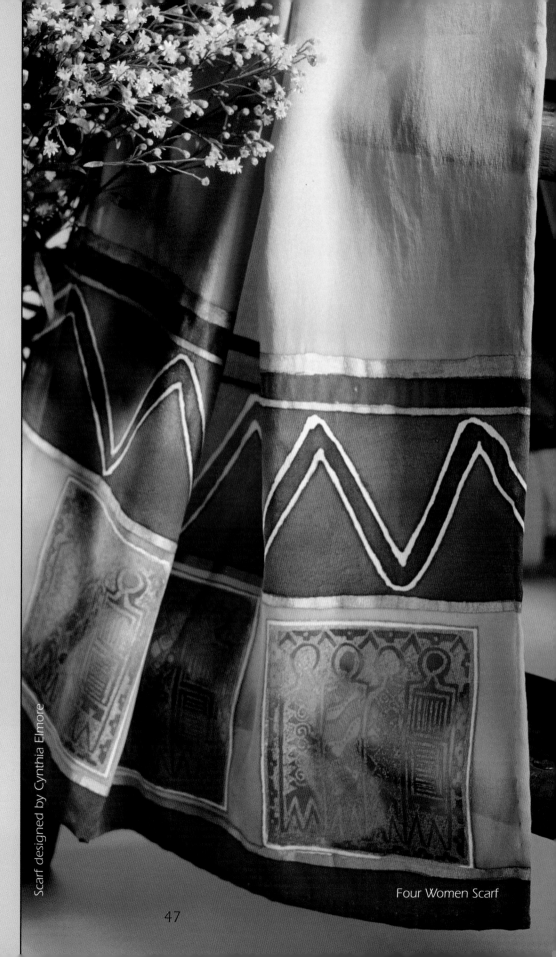

Scarf designed by Cynthia Elmore

Four Women Scarf

petroglif scarf

designed by Cynthia Elmore
See photo on page 124.

materials:

fabric dyes: dk. blue-green; brass; brown;
   dk. brown; lt. gray-yellow; ochre; bright
   orange; yellow-green
fabric inks for stamping: black; blue-purple;
   burgundy; chocolate; lemon yellow; med.
   orange; red-orange; yellow-green
fabric paint: gold acrylic
frame: stretcher bars or wood strips (slightly
   larger than fabric)
paintbrushes: watercolor, sm.; med.; lg.
plastic squeeze applicators: for resists and
   gold paint (3)
resist: black gutta; water-soluble
rubber stamps: bird head; lg. deer; sm. deer;
   lg. goat; sm. goat; lg. spiral; sm. spiral; sun
   symbol
scarf fabric: moss green, 37" square
thread: coordinating

implements:

bleach (optional)
embossing heat gun (optional)
iron and ironing board
paper: 37" square (2)
push pins
sewing machine

instructions:

Refer to **general instructions** on pages 8–10.

1. Lay out design on paper to determine placement of black resist lines to simulate cracks which might be found in a sheer rock wall. Position rubber stamps and determine where to add color to fabric. Keep this pattern near work area for reference.

2. Wash fabric. Attach dry fabric to frame using push pins so fabric is suspended above work surface. *Note: Frame can be made from wood strips. Smaller projects can use a high-sided cardboard box with dimensions slightly larger than fabric.*

3. Using black gutta resist, apply lines. Using water-soluble resist, apply lines. This creates boundaries for brushing on lines of color. Make certain there are no gaps or broken lines in resist lines. Let resists dry thoroughly.

4. Using paintbrushes and fabric dye, paint colors on design as desired. Let dye dry thoroughly. *Note: Embossing heat gun will speed this process.*

5. Remove fabric from frame. Place fabric under paper to protect gutta. Using iron and ironing board, heat set color by ironing three minutes at temperature setting suited for fabric.

6. Using warm water, wash out clear resist from fabric. Black resist will not be affected. Attach wet fabric back onto frame using push pins. *Optional: An extremely diluted solution of bleach may be applied at this time to lighten selected areas of fabric before dyeing.*

7. While fabric is wet, paint dye colors on design as desired. Refer to pattern made at beginning of project. Work within black resist lines to create a wash of color within each area. *Note: If fabric begins to dry out, use lg. paintbrush and wet only the area being worked. Avoid reworking dry areas as this will cause water spots to form on fabric.*

8. After all areas are complete, let fabric dry thoroughly. Using gold acrylic fabric paint, apply highlights as desired along cracks.

9. Remove fabric from frame. Place fabric under paper and heat set color by ironing as before.

10. Place fabric on flat surface with a layer of paper beneath. Using rubber stamps and fabric ink, stamp designs onto fabric as desired. Brush color accents onto stamped images using fabric dye. After all areas are complete, let fabric dry thoroughly. Heat set color by ironing as before.

11. Machine-stitch narrow hem along scarf edges.

special care:
Hand wash scarf very carefully. Press on low setting. Use ironing cloth or clean paper between iron and fabric to protect resist.

Cynthia Elmore, well-known illustrator and designer, has been associated for over 10 years with Personal Stamp Exchange, a leader in the collectable rubber stamp industry. Her beautifully detailed designs are familiar to rubber stamp aficionados world wide.

For a number of years Cynthia's illustrations were posted from remote islands in the tropics. She worked and traveled under sail from San Francisco to Tahiti, west through Pacific backwaters such as Fiji, Samoa, the Marshals and the Solomons, and down to New Zealand and Australia.

Travel and photography keep her busy when she has no commitments to stay home. She now resides in Sonoma County, California where she spends as much time as possible outdoors, hiking or biking between the redwoods and the ocean. She also loves to carve wood, paint furniture, and garden with the invaluable help of her inquisitive cats.

Cynthia's lifelong work as an artist began with her formal education at the University of North Carolina, continuing to a professional career first in design and fabrication of stained glass and sandblasted glass, then in commercial art. Most recently, Cynthia has focused her talents on rubber stamp design, craft project design, and painting in water media. Her contributions have played an important role in creating the elegant and classic look for which Personal Stamp Exchange is known. Many of her well-loved paintings have appeared on the covers of Personal Stamp Exchange catalogs.

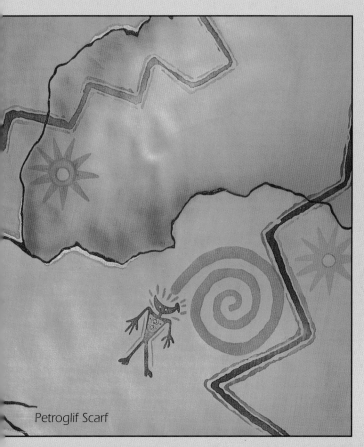

Petroglif Scarf

stamped country cat scarf

designed by Chapelle

materials:

acrylic paint: lt. brown, dk. green, lt. green,
    pink, white, dk. yellow
embossing powder: clear
fabric medium
fusible web: double sided
paint brush: small round
paper: white (size of cat stamp)
perle cotton, #8: black
pigment ink: black
rubber stamps: cat with fish, picket fence
scarf fabric: desired color and type, 13" x 6"
    for stamping; coordinating color and type,
    62" x 13"

implements:

craft scissors
heat tool
needles: embroidery

instructions:

Refer to **general instructions** on pages 8–10.

1. Find center of width of fabric for stamping
and mark.

2. Measure ½" up from bottom of one long side
of fabric and mark along the length.

3. Apply pigment ink to cat stamp. Center and
press stamp on fabric, aligning the bottom
edge of the stamp with the ½" mark.

4. Cover stamped image with embossing
powder and set with heat tool. Remove excess
powder.

5. To prepare for stamping the picket fence,
mask off cat by applying ink to cat stamp and
pressing image on white paper. Using craft
scissors, cut around outline of cat image. Place
the paper cat over the cat on fabric to protect it
from stamping that is to follow.

6. Apply pigment ink to picket fence stamp.

Holding the paper cat in place, press stamp on
fabric, slightly overlapping paper and on the
left side of cat on fabric. Repeat for the right
side of cat.

7. Cover stamped picket fence image with
embossing powder and set with heat tool.
Remove excess powder.

8. Thin acrylic paints with water and fabric
medium. Paint cat and fence design as desired.

9. Cut fusible web to 13" x 6" and, following
manufacturer's instructions, iron web to wrong
side of stamped fabric. Trim fused fabric to 5" x
13". Remove paper backing and align fused
fabric with one short end of coordinating
fabric. Iron to fuse both fabrics together.

10. Complete a ¼" turned hem on all scarf
edges except the stamped edge. Refer to
ribbon embroidery stitches on page 54. Using
black perle cotton, work evenly spaced buttonhole stitches along stamped edge of scarf.

block stamped sunflower scarf

designed by Chapelle

materials:

acrylic paint: black, dk. brown, bright true blue, maroon, lt. olive green, dk. olive green, dk.yellow, med. yellow, lt. yellow

block stamps: checkerboard, sunflower

fabric pen: .05 brown

paint brushes: ¼" flat, fine script

scarf fabric: desired color and type, 45" x 45"

implements:

palette sheet: all-purpose, disposable

instructions:

Refer to **general instructions** on pages 8–10.

1. Square fabric and mark fringe depth on all four sides by pulling threads. Machine-stitch just within this mark.

2. Squeeze small amount of brown acrylic paint onto disposable palette.

3. Lightly tap sunflower center block stamp into brown paint, making certain entire shape is evenly covered. Stamp, by pressing paint side down, onto fabric.

4. Squeeze small amounts of dk., med., and lt. yellow onto palette. Tap sunflower petal block stamps into colors, mixing paint on the shape itself. Stamp onto fabric around brown center. Apply fresh paint to block stamp after each stamping. Repeat around center until flower is complete.

5. Repeat Step 4 with dk. and lt. olive green paint, using leaf block stamps.

6. Using fine script paint brush and dk. olive paint, lightly draw in stems.

7. Using flat paint brush, carefully brush blue paint onto checkerboard block stamp. Stamp onto fabric near sunflower.

8. Using tip of paint brush handle, dot dk. brown paint onto center of sunflower.

9. Draw light lines into sunflower petals with script brush and lt. yellow paint.

10. Using .05 fabric pen, outline design and add "stitch" marks.

11. Finish scarf by pulling threads around outer edges to stitching.

stenciled scarf

designed by Chapelle
See photo on opposite page.

materials:
acrylic paints: dk. brown; copper metallic; gold metallic
scarf fabric: 30" square
sponges (3)
stencils: pre-cut
textile medium
thread: gold metallic (3 spools)

implements:
iron and ironing board
masking tape
old newspapers
palette sheet: all-purpose, disposable
paper towels
rubbing alcohol
scrap paper
sewing machine

instructions:
Refer to **general instructions** on pages 8–10.

1. Using 1" square of masking tape, mark center of scarf.

2. Place and tape stencil onto scarf for desired design.

3. Using paper palette, prepare mixture of each color of acrylic paint and textile medium following manufacturer's instructions.

4. Dampen sponges. Using paper towels, remove excess water from sponges. *Note: Practice design on scrap paper before beginning project.* Dip sponge into dk. brown mixture. Stencil onto scarf fabric. Let paint dry for a few minutes. Repeat process using gold metallic mixture, then copper metallic mixture. *Note: For a more subtle effect, stencil-paint and layer while still wet.* Let paints dry thoroughly. Remove stencil and work next area of design.

5. Using sewing machine and gold metallic thread, hem all edges of scarf using satin stitch. This may be sewn in free machine embroidery or set for regular stitching. Set stitch width as desired. Move fabric slowly so the stitches lie next to each other. Repeat.

Note: Stencils should be cleaned thoroughly using rubbing alcohol if they are to be used as a reverse design.

special care:
Spot clean scarf. Dry clean if necessary.

Stenciled Scarf

ribbon techniques for scarves

buttonhole stitch

1. Bring needle up at a, down at b. Bring needle up again at c, keeping ribbon under needle.

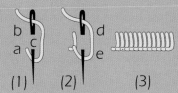

2. For second stitch, go down at d and back up at e. Continue in same manner.

3. Completed buttonhole stitches.

cascading

1. Stitch or glue bow knot to fabric. Thread ribbon streamer on needle. Allow ribbon to twist. Go down at a.

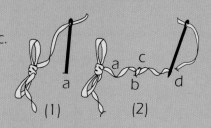

2. Come up at b and down at c, making a small backstitch to hold cascade in place. Come up at d. Repeat for desired length for cascading.

feather stitch

1. Come up at a, go down at b. Come back up at c, keeping ribbon under needle to hold in a "V" shape. Pull flat.

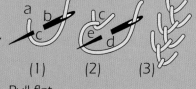

2. For second stitch, go down at d; back up at e.

3. Completed feather stitch.

herringbone stitch

1. Work stitch from right to left. Bring needle up at a, go down at b. Bring needle up at c, taking a small horizontal backstitch. Continue working, alternating from side to side for completed herringbone stitch.

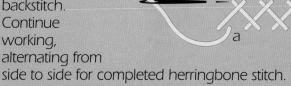

knotted mum stitch

1. Bring ribbon up through fabric. At ¼"-½" from entry point, tie knot.

2. Fold ribbon over on itself, forming a loop and go down into fabric at base of loop.

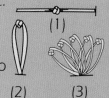

3. Place stitches close together for completed knotted mum stitches.

lazy daisy stitch

1. Bring needle up at a. Keep ribbon flat, untwisted and full. Put needle down at b and up at c, keeping ribbon under needle to form a loop. Pull ribbon through, leaving loop in place, go down on other side of ribbon near c, forming a straight stitch over loop.

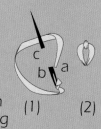

2. Completed lazy daisy.

lazy daisy stitch, cross-over

1. Bring needle up at a. Cross over to right of ribbon, go down at b and come back up at c, pulling ribbon to desired shape.

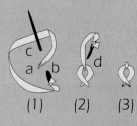

2. Go down at d, making a straight stitch to tack loop.

3. Completed cross-over lazy daisy stitch.

pointed petal leaf

1. Overlap ends of ribbon.

2. Gather-stitch at bottom edge.

3. Gather tightly to form petal. Wrap thread around stitches to secure. Trim excess ⅛" past stitching for completed pointed petal leaf.

ribbon flower

1. Fold ribbon in half along frayed edges, placing front ribbon edge slightly lower than back ribbon edge. Press at fold only. Gather-stitch ribbon.

2. Pull gathers tight and secure thread. Join ends. Completed ribbon flower.

ribbon stitch

1. Come up through fabric at starting point of stitch. Lay ribbon flat on fabric. At end of stitch, pierce ribbon with needle. Slowly pull length of ribbon through to back, allowing ends of ribbon to curl.

2. Completed ribbon stitch.

ribbon stitch, 1-twist

1. Follow (1) instructions for ribbon stitch twisting ribbon before pushing the needle back down.

2. Completed 1-twist ribbon stitch.

ribbon stitch, long, 1-twist

1. Follow (1) instructions for ribbon stitch, adding a twist in ribbon and taking a longer stitch before pushing the needle back down.

2. Completed long, 1-twist, ribbon stitch.

ribbon stitch, twisted & tacked

1. Follow (1) instructions for ribbon stitch, twisting ribbon before pushing the needle back down.

2. Come up at a, go down at b, tacking stitch, Completed twisted & tacked ribbon stitch.

rosette

1. Beginning at one end, fold end forward at right angle. Fold vertical end of ribbon forward upon itself.

2. Fold horizontal end of ribbon back and at right angle. Fold vertical ribbon over once. Continue folding ribbon back and over forming the rosette.

3. Upon reaching center mark, secure with a stitch, leaving needle and thread attached. Gather-stitch bottom edge of remaining ribbon. Gather tightly. Wrap gathered ribbon around bud.

4. Completed rosette.

stem stitch

1. Working from left to right, make slightly slanting stitches along line of stem. Come up at a, go down at b. Bring needle up at c and down at d. Continue in same manner for completed stem stitch.

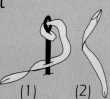

whip stitch

1. Use a single strand of thread knotted at one end. Insert needle at a, pick up a few threads of both layers, bringing needle out at b.

Scarves designed by Mary Jo Hiney

Wisteria Scarf

Flower & Vine Scarf

56

Lace Scarf

flower & vine scarf

designed by Mary Jo Hiney
See photo on page 56.

materials:

bias ribbons: 1"-wide, purple hand-dyed,
1¾ yds.; olive green hand-dyed, ¾ yd.
floss: silvery lilac, 2¾ yds.; moss; teal, 2¼ yds.
each
scarf fabric: 36" or 44"-wide, silk jacquard,
silvery lilac, 25" square
thread: coordinating

implements:

iron and ironing board
masking tape
needles: hand-sewing
ruler or tape measure
scissors: fabric
sewing machine
straight pins

instructions:

Refer to **general instructions** on pages 8–10
and **ribbon techniques for scarves** on pages
54–55.

1. Machine-stitch narrow hem along all edges
of scarf fabric.

2. To make cording for scarf vine, cut two 41"
lengths from each shade of floss. Hold one
length from each shade of floss together and
tie a knot in one end. Tape knotted end to
work surface. Tightly twist floss. Fold twisted
floss in half. Floss will double twist on itself,
creating cording for scarf vine. Knot ends
together. Repeat for remaining lengths of floss.

3. Pin cording to scarf for vine, placing finished
ends at one corner.

4. Using two strands of silvery lilac floss,

needle, and thread, hand-stitch vine to scarf.
Cut seven 8" lengths from purple ribbon. Run
fingernail along both edges to fray edges.
Make seven ribbon flowers.

5. Pin flowers onto vine. Hand-stitch flowers at
gathered centers to scarf vine.

6. Fray one edge of olive green ribbon. Cut
seven 4" lengths of olive green ribbon. Make
seven pointed petal leaves, having bias edge
outwards.

7. Press folded edges. Pin one leaf underneath
each flower. Hand-stitch to scarf at gathered
edge of leaf. Tack flower over leaf, hiding
gathered edge. Press vine, flowers, leaves,
and scarf.

special care:

Dry clean scarf. Can be pressed.

wisteria scarf

designed by Mary Jo Hiney
See photo on page 56.

materials:

floss: khaki brown; lt. brown, ½ yd. each
pens: dual tip blender, water-based;
med. blue; blush; lt. brown; med. brown;
burgundy; dk. burgundy; lt. gray;
med. gray; dk. green; med. green; peach;
bright pink; lt. pink; med. pink; dk. purple;
dk. yellow-brown; lt. yellow-brown; yellow-
gold; dk. yellow-gold
scarf fabric: 44"-wide, silk charmeuse,
khaki green, 2 yds.
silk ribbons: 4mm brown, 3½ yds.; dk. green,
3½ yds.; lt. green, 6 yds; khaki green,
2½ yds.; lt. purple, 1 yd.; purple-gray,
4½ yds; lt. rose, 3 yds.; white, 6 yds.;
pale yellow, 6 yds.
thread: coordinating

implements:

iron and ironing board
needles: embroidery, size 3; hand-sewing
needlework frame
paper towels
plastic cups: (6)
salt
scissors: fabric
sewing machine

instructions:

Refer to **general instructions** on pages 8–10 and **ribbon techniques for scarves** on pages 54–55.

1. To dye silk ribbons, fill plastic cups halfway with cold water. Pour ¼ cup salt into each cup and dissolve salt.

2. Remove one 3 yd. length of lt. green and lt. rose ribbon and two 3 yd. lengths of white and pale yellow ribbon from packages. Place one 3 yd. length in each cup. Let soak for ten minutes.

3. Place paper towels on work surface. Remove one 3 yd. length of ribbon from cup. Squeeze liquid from ribbon, open up, and lay flat on paper towel.

4. Immediately dye ribbons using pens. To dye ribbons using pens, begin with first shade, skipping it along the ribbon and leaving space for the other shades. Repeat with remaining shades. Lightly coat entire ribbon with blender pen. Set ribbon aside onto paper towel to dry for ten minutes. Continue until all six shades of ribbon have been dyed.

5. Using lt. green ribbon, dye with med. green, med. blue, dk. green, and lt. yellow-brown pens to make green hand-dyed ribbon. Using lt. rose ribbon, dye with blush, lt. gray, med. gray, and lt. pink pens to make blush hand-dyed ribbon.

6. Using one 3 yd. length of white ribbon, dye with bright pink, med. pink, burgundy, and dk. yellow-brown pens to make bright pink hand-dyed ribbon.

7. Using one 3 yd. length of white ribbon, dye with med. brown, dk. burgundy, dk. purple, and dk. yellow-brown pens to make purple hand-dyed ribbon.

8. Using one 3 yd. length of pale yellow ribbon, dye with bright pink, med. pink, burgundy, and dk. yellow-brown pens to make bright rose hand-dyed ribbon.

9. Using one 3 yd. length of pale yellow ribbon, dye with peach, lt. gray, yellow-gold, and dk. yellow-gold pens to make gold hand-dyed ribbon.

10. Place all six shades of ribbon in the six cups of salted water again and soak for five minutes. Rinse each shade in fresh, cold water until color runs clear. Squeeze liquid from ribbon. Set hand-dyed ribbons aside onto paper towel. Let dry for 15 minutes. Press with hot iron. Using fabric scissors, cut one piece of silk charmeuse fabric for scarf 11" x 60" along bias. Cut scarf lining piece 11" x 58" along bias. Keep scarf ends pointed.

11. Embroider design following **wisteria embroidery stitch guide** and **wisteria embroidery placement diagram** on page 60. *Note: To keep embroidery taut while stitching, mount area to be embroidered onto needlework frame. After embroidery is complete, use ironing board and steam iron to block embroidery.*

12. Machine-stitch scarf sides to lining, right sides together, leaving pointed ends free. Machine-stitch narrow hem along pointed ends of scarf and scarf lining fabrics. Press as

needed, keeping iron away from ribbon embroidery. Do not press scarf side seams.

special care:
Spot clean scarf. Dry clean as last resort. Do not press flat.

wisteria embroidery stitch guide

description	ribbon or floss	stitch
wisteria stems	lt. brown floss (2 strands)	stem stitch
leaf spray stems	khaki brown floss (2 strands)	stem stitch
wisteria, top layers	purple hand-dyed, purple-gray, brown	lazy daisy stitch
wisteria, top layers	purple hand-dyed, purple-gray, brown	ribbon stitch; ribbon stitch, 1-twist
daisy	gold, blush, bright rose, bright pink hand-dyed	knotted mum stitch
leaf spray leaves	green hand-dyed, lt. green, dk. green	lazy daisy stitch, cross-over
leaves	green hand-dyed, khaki green	ribbon stitch, 1-twist

wisteria embroidery placement diagram   enlarge 155%

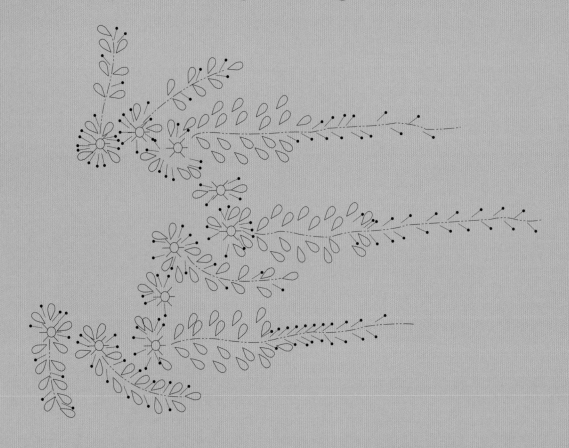

lace scarf

designed by Mary Jo Hiney
See photo on page 57.

materials:

beads: 14/0 seed, yellow-gray (1 pkg.);
   11/0 antique seed, silver (40);
   4mm antique round, pink pearl (5)
buttons: ¼"-wide vintage, mother-of-pearl (9)
lace: vintage ivory, vintage ecru, 3"-12",
   8-9 different types, shapes, and sizes,
   one piece must have a corner;
   2½"-wide vintage ivory, ½ yd. (2)
lace edging: ⅛"-wide vintage ivory, 1 yd.;
   ⅜"-wide ivory, 2¼ yds.
scarf fabric: 44"-wide China silk, ivory,
   9" x 52"
silk ribbons: 4mm, ivory; blush; pale peach;
   white; pale gold; ecru; dk. ecru, ½-1 yd.
   each
thread: ivory

implements:

iron and ironing board
needles: beading; hand-sewing
scissors: fabric
sewing machine

instructions:

Refer to **general instructions** on pages 8–10
and **ribbon techniques for scarves** on pages
54–55.

1. Using fabric scissors, cut silk fabric 9" x 52".
Square off one scarf end, keeping other end
pointed.

2. Press vintage laces. Beginning with corner
shaped lace piece, pin laces to pointed end of
scarf, overlapping laces ¼". Use curved lace
pieces for bridging gaps along outer edges.

3. Using hand-sewing needle and ivory thread,
whip-stitch lace pieces to scarf. Press as needed.

4. Turn scarf edges under to match shape of
lace at each point. Whip-stitch turned under
fabric to lace at all areas possible. Some laces
will not have a finished edge at scarf edge.

5. Machine-stitch narrow hem along remaining
scarf edges, including squared-off end. Overlap
and stitch 2½"-wide laces to squared off scarf
end. Turn cut edges of lace under at hemmed
scarf edges and whip stitch. At scarf end, turn
under any laces not finished and whip-stitch.

6. Whip-stitch edge of ⅛"-wide vintage lace
edging to outer edge of appliqued lace.
Whip-stitch edge of ⅜"-wide lace edging to
straight edges of scarf.

7. Cut one 18" length from pale peach and
blush ribbons. Set aside for bows.

8. Use purchased silk flowers or make rosettes.
To make rosettes, cut 5" lengths from ribbon as
follows: three ivory, two blush, one pale peach,
two white, three pale gold, three ecru, and
three dk. ecru. Make each length into a rosette.
Randomly place and hand-stitch rosettes to
lace.

9. Using each 18" length from pale peach and
blush ribbon, tie a tiny bow at center of each
length. Hand-stitch bows near a rosette.
Cascade-stitch ribbon ends.

10. Cluster and hand-stitch beads and buttons
to appliqued lace.

special care
Hand wash scarf in cold water. Block lace. Do
not press ribbon.

Scarf designed by MaryJo Hiney

Crazy Quilt Scarf

crazy quilt scarf

designed by Mary Jo Hiney
See photo on opposite page.

materials:

beads: #5 bugle, bronze (2 pkgs.);
   #5 bugle, indigo (2 pkgs.);
   14/0 seed, bright burgundy (1 pkg.);
   11/0 seed, indigo (1 pkg.);
   11/0 antique seed, silver (2 pkgs.);
   11/0 antique seed, gold (2 pkgs.);
   3.5mm round, antique pearl; ecru (2 pkgs.);
   4mm round, pink (4)
chenille: 1/16"-wide bronze, 1 yd.
floss: silk, blush; ecru; gold; lt. gold; lt. purple;
   bright rose (1 pkg. each)
lace: 3"-wide, vintage brown, 1/2 yd. (2)
scarf fabric: 36"-60"-wide velvet, brown,
   36" square; crazy quilt, assorted scraps,
   6" x 9" (12); 36"-wide China silk, neutral,
   3/4 yd. for base cloth
silk ribbons: 4mm dk. burgundy, 7 yds.;
   sea green; dk. rose, 2 yds. each;
   taupe, 1 1/4 yds.; orange-gold, 1/2 yd;
   7mm lt. burgundy; dk. red, 1 1/4 yds. each;
   variegated dk. green, 2 1/2 yds.
thread: coordinating

implements:

iron and ironing board
needles: beading; chenille, size 20;
   embroidery, size 3; hand-sewing
scissors: fabric
sewing machine
straight pins

Crazy Quilt Scarf close-up

instructions:

Refer to **general instructions** on pages 8–10
and **ribbon techniques for scarves** on pages
54–55.

1. Transfer **base cloth pattern** on page 65 onto
China silk fabric. Using fabric scissors, cut out
pattern.

2. Trim two scrap pieces of crazy quilt fabric in
random sizes, having one edge of each piece
the same length. Machine-stitch onto base
cloth, right sides together, taking 1/4" seam along
same-size edge. Open out and press.

3. Vary fabric piece choices and continue to
stitch different sized crazy quilt pieces onto
each other, right sides together. Keep different
sized pieces 6" x 3". Trim outer edges to fit
desired shape or area after piecing is finished.
Overlap brown lace over some scrap pieces. Fill
entire base cloth with assorted scrap pieces.
Open out pieces and press after each seam.

4. Using chenille needle, stitch crazy quilting by alternating silk floss and stitches with feather, buttonhole, and herringbone stitches. Embroider ribbon design onto crazy quilting following crazy quilt embroidery stitch guide on opposite page. Refer to **crazy quilt placement diagram** on opposite page. Use chenille needle for 7mm ribbon and embroidery needle for 4mm ribbon.

5. Using beading needle, add beading to embroidery and crazy quilting as desired.

6. Using hand-sewing needle and coordinating thread for chenille vines, drape, pin, and tack chenille to crazy quilting with beads.

7. Cut five 3" circles from fabric scraps to make yo-yos. Allow ¼" seam allowance. Stitch gathering stitch ¼" along circumference of each circle. Draw up circles and tuck raw edges into center of yo-yos. Press flat with the gathering. Make a total of five yo-yos. Tack to crazy quilting. Using 7mm variegated dk. green ribbon and lazy daisy stitch, make desired number of pointed petal leaves and stitch around yo-yos as desired. Tack yo-yos to tip of leaves.

8. Embellish outer edges of yo-yos with indigo seed beads. Stitch 4mm round pink beads in center of each yo-yo.

9. Pin right side of crazy quilted piece to wrong side of brown velvet in one corner. Machine-stitch together, taking ½" seam. Trim seam at corner point. Turn right side of crazy quilted

piece over onto right side of brown velvet. Baste-stitch close to edge. Press. Hand-stitch narrow rolled hem along remaining scarf edges.

10. Whip-stitch basted scarf edge with dk. burgundy 4mm ribbon, placing stitches ¼" apart. Hide knots for entry points and ends.

11. Turn under top edge of crazy quilting ½" and hand-stitch to velvet fabric. Alternate silk floss and feather, buttonhole, and herringbone stitches to embroider top edge of crazy quilting and velvet fabric.

12. Double and knot thread onto beading needle. Stitch thread into scarf at bottom of crazy quilt corner, hiding knot. Slip three vintage silver beads, one bronze bugle bead, one bright burgundy seed bead, one bronze bugle bead, one antique ecru pearl, and one bright burgundy seed bead onto needle. Stitch back up through all beads except bottom seed bead. Stitch into scarf seam, pulling thread tight. Stitch to next whip stitch. Repeat, alternating indigo bugle beads for bronze bugle beads at every other row of fringe. Continue making beaded fringe up to end of crazy quilting seam.

13. For remaining edge of scarf, alternate three antique gold beads, three indigo bugle beads, one vintage ecru pearl, and one bright burgundy seed bead.

special care:
Dry clean scarf.

crazy quilt embroidery stitch guide

description	ribbon	stitch
mums, bottom layer	7mm dk. red	knotted mum stitch
mums, top layer	7mm lt. burgundy	knotted mum stitch
mum stamens	4mm taupe	ribbon stitch, 1-twist
mum stamens	4mm orange-gold	ribbon stitch, 1-twist
mum leaves, stems	7mm variegated dk. green	lazy daisy stitch; ribbon stitch, twisted & tacked; ribbon stitch, 1-twist
vines	chenille	
buds along vine	4mm dk. rose	lazy daisy stitch
leaves along vine	4mm sea green	ribbon stitch, 1-twist

base cloth pattern

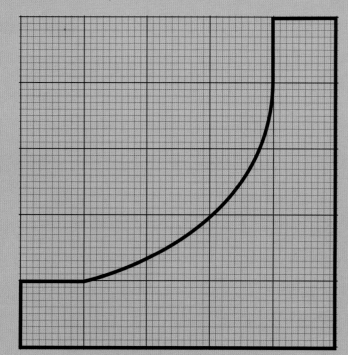

each 10 count grid equals 5"

crazy quilt placement diagram
enlarge 170%

dyeing & painting scarves

dyeing technique

Before starting a project, experiment on small pieces of fabric to see how the dyes and paints react. Dyes spread quickly and blending will occur. When dyeing fabric, work in a well-ventilated room and wear rubber gloves.

materials:
acid dyes
fabric paints
paintbrush: 3-stem bamboo
scarf fabric

implements:
2-qt. bucket
drop cloth
plastic containers
plastic garbage bag or sheeting: lg. enough
   to cover and protect work surface
rubber gloves

There are two methods for dyeing fabric. Choose the method that is most comfortable and convenient. Then, cover working surface using plastic (garbage bag or plastic sheeting) and place a drop cloth on top of plastic.

method one (fabric paint) instructions:
1. Using fabric paint, set up required number of plastic containers for each paint color. Use one plastic container for water to wet and rinse paintbrush.

2. Fill 2-qt. bucket with fresh cool water. Dip fabric into bucket of water until thoroughly wet. Remove fabric and squeeze out excess water. Open out fabric on working surface and check that all areas are wet. Rewet if necessary.

3. Wearing rubber gloves, follow project instructions for dyeing fabric using fabric paint.

method two (acid dye) instructions:
1. Using acid dye, fill 2-qt. bucket with fresh cool water. Prepare dye in bucket following manufacturer's instructions.

2. Wearing rubber gloves, dye fabric following manufacturer's instructions. Remove fabric and squeeze out excess water. Open fabric out on working surface and check that all areas are wet. Rewet if necessary.

3. Follow individual project instructions for embellishing.

painting technique

It is important to have all supplies ready as the dye cannot be allowed to dry on silk scarf between colors.

Before starting a project, experiment on small pieces of fabric to see how the dyes and paints react. Dyes spread quickly and blending will occur. When dyeing fabric, work in a well-ventilated room and wear rubber gloves.

materials:
cork adhesive and strips
dyes: suitable for silk
fabric pen
frame: stretcher bars, wood strips, or foam
   board (slightly larger than scarf fabric)
paintbrushes: round, sm; med.; lg.;
   foam, one for each dye color
resist: gutta; water-soluble
scarf fabric
sodium alginate thickener

implements:

canner: large for "home steamer"
cotton swabs for painting (optional)
foil: heavy
metal cylinder (#303 can with both ends
   cut out)
newspapers; pellon; old towels
packaging tape
pie plate
plastic cups
rubber gloves
straight pins: lg. with plastic heads

There are four methods for painting silk. Before the silk may be painted on, it must be stretched on frame.

1. Assemble frame. If using wood, place cork strips around frame using cork adhesive.

2. Stretch fabric across frame and secure with straight pins.

3. Mix each color of dye in separate paper cup. Decide on desired method listed on the following page.

method one (washed background) instructions:

1. To create a background of washed color gradation, dilute each color of dye with water in a plastic cup. The amount of water used will determine softness of color. It is best to use colors in an order that will blend well together. Use a foam brush for each different color.

2. Start at outside edge of fabric and brush around edge with desired color. Keep applying dye until desired color is achieved. Immediately apply next color, overlapping the first color. Continue until the center of fabric is reached.

For a long thin scarf, wash colors across from top to bottom. Let fabric dry thoroughly.

3. For a solid washed background, use only one color. Make certain enough diluted dye has been prepared for entire scarf, otherwise color may not be consistent. Let fabric dry thoroughly.

method two (wet on dry) instructions:

1. Using fabric pen, draw desired design onto fabric. Apply resist around design and let dry thoroughly. This procedure allows painting within lines without any bleeding of colors.

2. Paint onto dry fabric within the resist lines with a less diluted dye mixture.

method three (wet on wet) instructions:

To create a design that is more muted and abstract, paint within resist lines after wetting fabric small sections at a time. Use a foam brush to wet area before applying dye.

method four (discharging) instructions:

1. To create a design by removing color from the washed background, a color and dye remover may be used. Read and follow manufacturer's instructions.

2. Add small amount of sodium alginate thickener to thicken color remover in order to be able to paint on design. Read and follow manufacturer's instructions.

3. Paint this mixture onto scarf in design pattern desired. This mixture may also be used to correct mistakes by removing unwanted dye.

4. Fabric must be steamed to remove color.

steaming:

All silk fabric painted with silk dye must be steamed to set the color.

1. Roll pieces of silk in newsprint or pellon and tape securely.

2. To make a "home steamer" place large canner containing 1" of water over low heat on stove.

3. Place a metal cylinder (#303 can with both ends cut out) into steamer. Set a pie plate or flat lid on top of cylinder.

4. Place silk bundle onto plate, allowing plenty of space between sides and top of canner. Create an "umbrella" using heavy foil over silk bundle to prevent condensation from wetting silk. Do not wrap foil tightly.

5. Place an old towel between top of steamer and lid to absorb steam.

6. Place weight, such as an inverted heavy pan, on lid to retain steam.

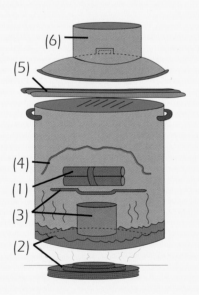

Steam silk for approximately one hour, or follow dye manufacturer's instructions.

Remove silk from steamer and unroll bundle. Let silk cure for approximately 12 hours. Rinse silk and let dry thoroughly.

Dry clean silk to remove gutta resist. *Note: There are water-soluble resists that may be used and dry cleaning is not necessary.* If water-soluble resist is used, hand wash silk in hot water using mild dishwashing liquid. Rinse, then press while still damp.

adding metallic & other bold accents

1. Restretch finished scarf onto frame. Using stiff watercolor brush and metallic fabric paint (or fabric paint of choice) add designs and highlights as desired.

2. Fabric paint must be heat set. Place fabric in dryer on hottest setting for approximately 40 minutes. *Note: Commercial dryers are often hotter and may provide a better set.*

Another method to heat set is to use a hot iron (no steam) over painted areas by slowly pressing and lifting from each area to the next.

marble paint technique

Marbling designs may be done on fabric, paper, wood, or almost any porous material. Marbling kits available at craft stores consist of marbling concentrate powder, acrylic paint, eyedroppers, marbling combs, and instructions.

1. Read and follow manufacturer's instructions. Prepare marbling solution. Fabric dyes may be used and should be thinned.

2. Prewash all fabric. Fabric must be dry before it touches the paint or it will not absorb the color.

Scarf designed by Sarah Mays-Salin

69

Painted Scarf

painted scarf

desinged by Sarah Mays-Salin
See photo on page 69.

materials:

fabric paints: purple; dk. blue; lt. blue-green
paintbrush: 3-stem bamboo
scarf fabric: 55"-wide China silk, white, ½ yd.,
    torn so crosswise edges are on the grain

implements:

2-qt. bucket
drop cloth: 72" x ½ yd.
iron and ironing board
plastic containers: (5)
plastic garbage bag
rubber gloves

instructions:

Refer to **general instructions** on pages 8–10.

1. Wet fabric using method one, dyeing technique, page 66. Prepare working surface. Fold drop cloth several times to make an area 18" square of multiple layers for absorbency. Place fabric on working surface and working from the middle of fabric using both hands, begin scrunching up fabric to create little hills and valleys. Gradually work the whole piece of fabric until it is scrunched up to 12" x 8".

2. Dip paintbrush into water then into purple fabric paint. Touch paintbrush to fabric. Use a dabbing motion to paint "hilltops" or exposed surface of scrunched fabric. *Note: Do not saturate entire piece with one color. Allow each color to spread on its own onto white fabric and other paint colors.*

3. Dip paintbrush into water then into dk. blue fabric paint and follow same method around edges of fabric, covering 2" space from edge inward. Dab onto some "hilltops."

4. Dip and rinse paintbrush in water. Dip paintbrush into water then into lt. blue-green fabric paint and follow same method as a highlight on a few "hilltops". Using both hands, turn fabric over with as little disturbance to "landscape" as possible. If "landscape" is disturbed, scrunch up fabric again and continue painting around some, but not all, white areas on fabric.

5. When finished painting fabric, leave undisturbed 24 hours to dry thoroughly.

6. Clean paintbrush and plastic paint containers. Fabric paint may be placed in original container for later use.

7. When scarf has dried thoroughly, heat set scarf using iron following fabric paint manufacturer's instructions.

special care:

Hand wash scarf in lukewarm water using mild shampoo or mild detergent. Hang to dry.

textured scarf

desinged by Sarah Mays-Salin
See photo on page 72.

materials:

acid dye: emerald green
beads: 9/0 seed, hex 3-cut, lt. green (1 hank);
    4mm round, topaz (50); 4mm flat rondelles,
    purple iris (50)
fusible interfacing: gray
scarf fabric: China silk, mint green, 15" x 90"
    for scarf front; silk, coordinating or
    contrasting color, 10" x 60" for scarf back
thread: beading, white; sewing, coordinating

implements:

2-qt. bucket
drop cloth: cotton canvas, 72" x 1 yd.

iron and ironing board
needle: beading; hand-sewing
plastic sheeting: lg. enough to cover work
  surface
press cloth: cotton or muslin, 12" x 8"
rubber gloves
scissors: fabric
sewing machine

instructions:
Refer to **general instructions** on pages 8–10.

1. Fold fusible interfacing in half lengthwise. Using fabric scissors, cut on fold line. With right non-fusible sides together, machine-stitch short sides creating one long piece 12" x 72". Trim to final size of 10" x 60".

2. Dye fabric using method two, dyeing technique, page 66. Prepare working surface. Place fabric on working surface and working from the middle of fabric using both hands, begin scrunching up fabric to create little hills and valleys. Pinch, pleat, and wrinkle fabric in an irregular fashion. Gradually work entire piece of fabric until it is scrunched up to slightly larger than the size of prepared fusible interfacing. Check size by using fusible interfacing as a template. Avoid large folds or areas with too much or too little fabric. Arrange fabric in a true rectangle using fusible interfacing as a template.

Note: Ironing is to be done where project is set up on working surface. Using iron on steam setting, gently pat, one area at a time, along entire length of fabric. This is to flatten and dry fabric. Do not use force or weight on iron.

3. Place fusible interfacing out on scrunched fabric making final adjustments to fabric to fit size of interfacing. Fuse interfacing to fabric following manufacturer's instructions. Use wet press cloth, rewetting cloth for each area pressed.

4. Turn fabric over and press lightly. This will now be right side of scarf. Allow fabric to dry.

5. Using beading needle and thread, hand-stitch beads to front of fabric. Refer to **textured scarf beading diagrams** below. Use the folds of fabric to dictate placement of stems so they appear to emerge from under folds. Vary the length and direction of stems and stem groups to cover entire scarf front with a loose pattern of about 45 stem groups 3"-5" apart.

6. With right sides together, machine-stitch front to backing fabric. Leave an opening about 4" for turning. Trim edges to reduce bulk.

7. Turn fabric. Press with dry iron. Using hand-sewing needle and coordinating thread, blind-stitch opening closed.

special care:
Hand wash scarf in lukewarm water using mild shampoo. Lay flat to dry. Press scarf with textured side down on top of towel. Press lining side only.

textured scarf beading diagrams

Scarf designed by Sarah Mays-Salin

Textured Scarf

Sarah Mays-Salin was born and raised in Northern California, where she has lived most of her life. "I draw a lot of my inspiration from the natural beauty of this area and particularly the plant and insect kingdoms. I am also greatly influenced by the environment of my upbringing: my mother's nurturing openness to my creativity, and the inventive engineering of my father."

Sarah studied Fiber Art at the California College of Arts and Crafts and Pacific Basin Textile School. "I have been working with ribbon and fabric manipulation since 1988, spending most of my time as a designing craftsperson with stops along the way to do costuming for theater, and, not least, to become a wife and mother." Her work has been shown and sold across the U.S. and Japan.

Sarah's current work is the exploration of fabric manipulation techniques combined with painting to create wearable art and sculpture. "The process of creating from my intuitive observation, represents and helps me recognize and live my deep connection to the grace in nature."

Sarah has included additional photos of "gallery" scarves that demonstrate what can be accomplished after mastering this technique.

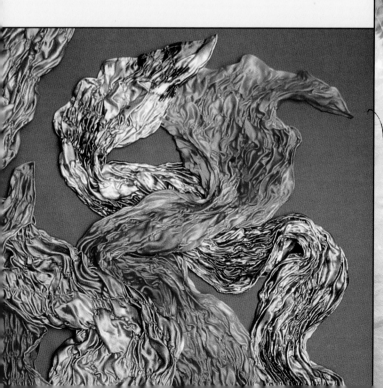

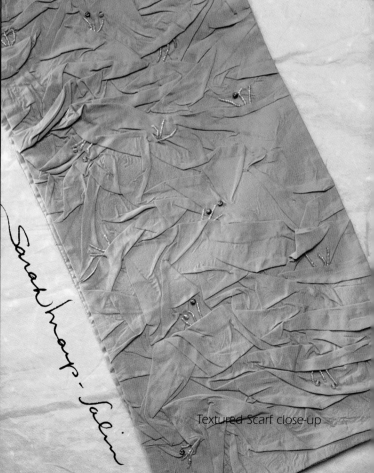

Textured Scarf close-up

silk painted scarf

desinged by Roberta Glidden
See photo on opposite page.

materials:

cork adhesive & strips
dyes
fabric paint: gold metallic
fabric pen: invisible
foam brushes: one for each dye color
frame: stretcher bars or wood strips
  (slightly larger than scarf fabric)
paintbrushes: round, size 10, 12, 14
scarf fabric: China silk or crepe, desired scarf
  size, or purchased blank scarf with finished
  hand-stitch narrow rolled hem
sodium alginate thickener
thread: coordinating for hemming

implements:

home steamer
iron and ironing board
sewing machine
plastic cups
rubber gloves
straight pins: lg. with plastic heads

instructions:

Refer to **general instructions** on pages 8–10.

1. Prepare dyes to be used using method one, paint technique, on pages 66–68 . Brush dye onto fabric, starting at outer edge. Model scarf colors are applied in the following order: dk. gray, lt. gray, mauve, tan; repeat. Let scarf dry thoroughly.

2. Pale gray squiggly lines and dots were created using method four, paint technique, on page 67. Draw design onto scarf using fabric pen.

3. Prepare color remover following manufacturer's instructions. Add small amount of sodium alginate to thicken. Paint mixture over design lines. *Note: Color will not disappear until scarf has been steamed.*

4. Draw additional designs onto dry fabric. Brush over design lines with less diluted mixtures of color used in washed background. Since model scarf is more of an abstract design, it is not necessary to use resist around design lines. Let scarf dry thoroughly.

5. Using home steamer, steam scarf. Wash, dry, and press scarf.

6. Stretch dry scarf back onto frame. Using gold metallic fabric paint, add highlights. Heat set fabric paint by placing in dryer on hottest setting for about 40 minutes. Another method is to use a hot iron, no steam, over painted areas by slowly pressing and lifting from each area to next.

7. Machine-stitch narrow hem along all scarf edges.

special care:

Hand wash or dry clean scarf. Iron on wrong side of scarf.

Scarves designed by Roberta Glidden   Model Ryanne Webster

Silk Painted Scarf

City, and her work appears in Volume II of Silk Painting For Fashion and Fine Art by Susan Moyer.

Roberta received her B.A. from the University of Colorado in 1967 and has studied art at Weber State University in Ogden as a graduate student. She has taught with the Utah Arts Council Artist in Education program since 1976 and has been on the arts faculty of the University of Utah Textile Arts Program. In 1991 she taught drawing on the fall voyage of Semester at Sea with the University of Pittsburgh.

Roberta Glidden

Pages 75–79 feature additional photos of "gallery" scarves that demonstrate what can be accomplished after mastering this technique.

Roberta Glidden, a Seattle, Washington native, has lived in Ogden, Utah since 1969 when she moved from Boulder, Colorado with her husband and baby son. Her growing interest in silk painting led her to buy her current studio space, an 80 year old bungalow which is lovingly restored where she works and also teaches...when she is not gardening or hiking in the desert.

Roberta was a founder of Utah Designer Crafts Gallery in downtown Salt Lake City, Utah and a co-owner for eight years. She has participated in several group and solo exhibits and received juror and purchase awards with the Utah Arts Council and the Eccles Community Arts Center for her silk paintings. She has exhibited in the national American Crafts Council Fairs and has recently shown work at the Utah Arts Festival, Pacific Northwest Arts and Crafts Fair (Bellevue, Washington) and the Park City Arts Festival.

She has designed two official scarves for the Salt Lake City Olympic Bid Committee, has worked with textile design studios in New York

Scarf designed by Roberta Glidden · Model Ryanne Webster

Scarf designed by Roberta Glidden • Model Ryanne Webster

Gail MacKenzie

Gail continues to work on the innovative technique of adding marbled patterns over hand-painted designs, or primary marble patterns, textures in the weave of the silk, and prints. "I like the dimension and the depth these designs have. I like the colors. A brand new palette of colors is the result."

Gail uses only the finest quality Italian, Korean, and some Chinese silks. She uses the techniques and traditional materials that marblers have used for centuries, as well as the latest available pigments and techniques. "Combining traditional marbling with other surface design methods, gives my work a special, very different look."

Gail MacKenzie studied art at San Diego University in California, where she received her B.A. degree. A working fabric artist for over 20 years, she is known internationally for her trend-setting designs.

Photos on the opposite page feature "gallery" scarves that demonstrate what can be accomplished after mastering marbelizing.

Scarf designed by Cynthia Wayne Gaffield / Model: Ruanne Webster

82

Cynthia Wayne Gaffield

"Dying silk is my passion," states **Cynthia Wayne Gaffield**, "with the colors bringing life to the majestic silk fibers." Studio Designer/Fiber Artist, Cynthia, is currently residing in Livonia, Michigan, with her husband, son, and cat. Her studio is located in nearby Farmington Hills. "I work with textured tussah silk," she continues, "incorporating intense hand-painted colors with geometric shaped patterns. Coats and scarves are designed of my fabrics, often embellished with semi-precious beads and hand-twisted fringe."

Cynthia's pieces are featured as "gallery" scarves and demonstrate what can be accomplished after mastering this technique.

Cynthia was educated in Fine Art and Graphic Design at Oakland Community College in Farmington Hills, Michigan. Since then, she has continued to keep her education current through design workshops sponsored by various universities and art organizations. Her designs have been appearing in exhibitions and trade shows nationwide since 1983.

"My work has primarily grown through self exploration. My interest in fibers explores the interaction of fabric, dye, and paint with texture. I thoroughly love what I do, and my work is represented by galleries and boutiques across the country."

83

Jan Mayer was born and educated in California where he graduated from San Diego State University with lifetime teaching credentials in English and Social Studies. Although Jan loved teaching, he decided to pursue his life-long dream: a five-year trip around the world! He was convinced he could finance his journey by making and selling crafts along the way. He sold virtually everything he owned and started his adventure with about $1,300 in travel money.

Jan's artistry took a turn when he first discovered the art of French Painting on Silk during a juried exhibition of his leather-work in Paris. "I had never seen anything so beautiful in my life!" He was later invited to enter into an association with an outstanding French silk painter, Christiane Boiral, "Kriska" to her friends, from whom he learned the craft. They soon moved their studio, now known as Kriska, from the remote village in the French Alps to the San Francisco Bay area, becoming one of the first silk painting studios in the United States. In 1990, Christiane returned to Paris to pursue a career of fine art painting. Jan now resides in Salt Lake City, Utah. While Jan receives most of the public recognition for the accolades of Kriska Silks, he credits his good friends, loved ones, teachers, and collaborating artists for their guidance and boundless artistic inspiration; namely: Gregg Blue, Lynne Andrews, Christiane Boiral, Jon Drayson, Beverly Lujan, Roberta Glidden, Sergio Lub, Charles Feil, and especially his parents for their unconditional love and support.

Scarf designed by Jan Mayer & Jon Drayson   Photographed by Ralph Gabriner   Model-Dawn Colombo

Jan Mayer

In the "Basque Country" of southwestern France, Jan began making leather bracelets, wallets, belts, handbags, and key chains. "The people loved seeing me create these objects from my old VW Van, which served as my home and studio. I vividly remember the incredible euphoria of creating and selling these first few pieces."

He states, "What has kept me in the arts more than any other single thing is the quality of the lifelong friendships and associations I have made with other artists. The more you know about the artist- their trials, tribulations, as well as their hopes, dreams, and lifestyle—the more you will appreciate their work."

Jan's pieces on pages 84–87 are featured as "gallery" scarves and demonstrate what can be accomplished after mastering this technique.

Kriska
Painting on Silk

Scarf designed by Jan Mayer   Photographed by Ralph Gabriner   Model Laura Caulfield

Scarf designed by Jan Mayer & Jon Drayson   Photographed by Ralph Gabriner   Model Dawn Columbo

Scarf designed by Jan Mayer   Photographed by Ralph Gabriner   Model Tracy Coogan

Scarf designed by Jan Mayer   Photographed by Ralph Gabriner   Model Rae Klein

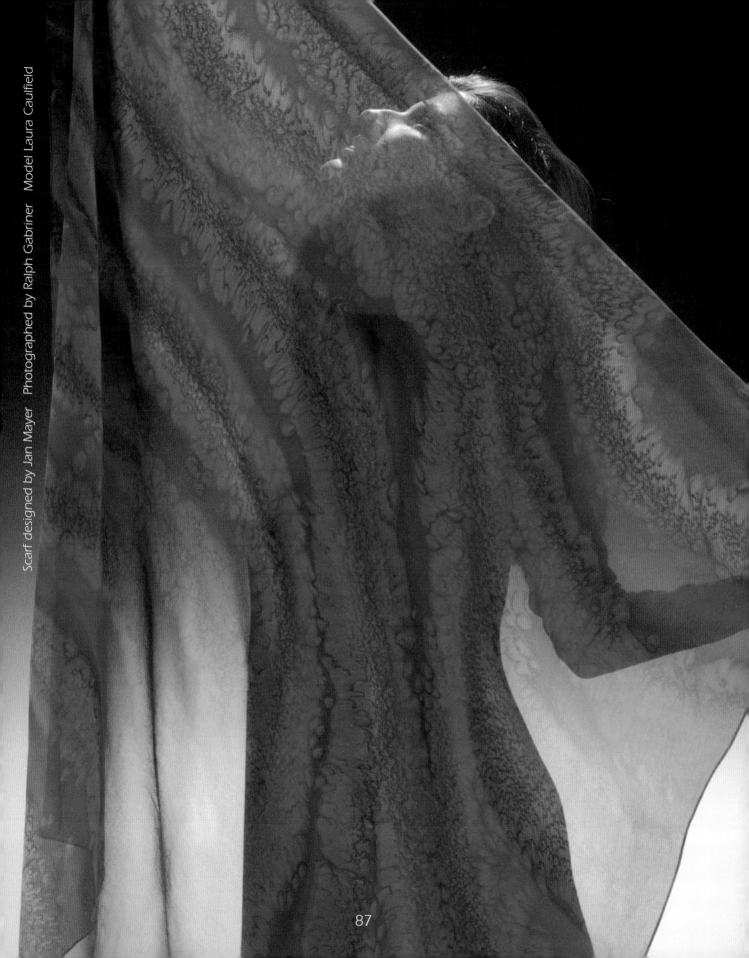

Scarf designed by Jan Mayer   Photographed by Ralph Gabriner   Model Laura Caulfield

Michael Davis has been doing pole-wrapped (bomaki) shibori since he took a workshop in "Japanese Dyeing Techniques" from Yoshiko Wada at Arrowmont Craft School in 1981.

"I remember walking through the teacher's exhibit when I arrived on the evening before the course and seeing an exhibit that Anna Headstrom had pole wrapped. I was blown away."

Because the resulting dye work can look and feel as if it is part of an ancient, timeless, Afro-Asian tradition of cloth, I have continued working with shibori. The textural pieces are allowed to dry after dyeing before being removed from the poles and must be kept dry to hold the texture.

Since 1995 I have been working with quilt artist **Carol Freeman**. Together we are "Shibori West" and our work is sold at about a dozen shops and galleries in the U.S. and Japan.

A life long attraction to color, pattern, and fiber combined with a Fine Arts and Textile Design degree brought Carol Freeman to pieced design for quilting.

"Painting with fabric and Shibari dyed silk is among the most beautiful," says Carol. "Each length of silk suggests its own color combination and pattern, and every scarf is unique. Their creation is a source of joy for me and they feel like pure luxury."

Pieces on pages 88–90 are featured as "gallery" scarves and demonstrate what can be accomplished after mastering this technique.

Scarf designed by Michael Davis and Carol Freeman   Model Karmen Quinney

Michael Davis
Carol Freeman

Scarf designed by Michael Davis and Carol Freeman Model Karmen Quinney

Yoriko Nishi is a graduate of Chicago's American Academy of Art, where she studied graphic art, illustration, oil-painting, water-color painting, and scratchboard art.

While pursuing a career as free-lance artist in the advertising industry for 20 years, Yoriko has continued her studies in fiber art, tie-dye, batik, marbleizing, silk-screening, and hand-painting silk.

"I find silk painting to be very challenging, yet satisfying due to the rich colors of dyes and flexibility of technique, as well as the beautiful texture of the fabric itself," states Yoriko. "My wearable creations represent simplicity, elegance, comfort, and timeless style."

Yoriko's surface designs are inspired by beauty of nature – predominantly florals, occasionally wildlife – combined with contemporary lines. Her decorative artwork is predominantly plant, flower, and animal oriented.

The artwork and designs of 'Yoriko' can be found currently on display at several prestigious fine art and fine craft shows across the country.

Yoriko's pieces on pages 91–92 are featured as "gallery" scarves and demonstrate what can be accomplished after mastering this technique.

weaving & knitting scarves

crayon box scarf

designed by Paula Chaffee Scardamalia
See photo on page 94.

materials:
dye fixative
yarn: rayon chenille at 1300 yd/lb, 1350 yds.
   total for warp, purple; blue; green; yellow;
   orange; red; 500 yds. total for weft (same 6
   colors); variegated rayon slub, 48 yds.
   optional

instructions:
Refer to **general instructions** on pages 8–10.

weave: plain weave.
finished dimension: 14" x 70", plus 4" fringe
   at each end.
epi: 15
ppi: 12
total warp ends: 225
warp length: 3½ yds. including take-up,
shrinkage, fringe, and 24" loom waste.
width & reed: 15"

1. Warp yarn at 15 epi starting with purple at
one edge, warp an average of 2" per color.
When moving from one color to next, warp
two colors together for several rounds before
dropping the previous color and continuing
with next color. Finish the warp by returning to
purple. Intermittently, wind in rayon slub as an
accent every couple of inches if desired.

2. Weave in a spacer for the fringe that is
washable, such as seam binding, for 6".
Beginning with purple weft, weave about 5"-
6". Repeat with blue, then green, yellow,
orange, red, back to purple for center, back to
red, orange, yellow, green, blue, finishing with
purple. Weave another 6" spacer at end for
fringe and then, when cutting from loom,
leave enough yarn to make overhand knots at
end of fringe to secure spacer. Repeat the
colors more than twice if desired, making the
blocks of color smaller or put small stripes of all
colors in middle block of purple. *Optional: Put
small bands of yellow or orange as a bright
accent in each of the blocks of color, or use
chenilles that have been spun with a glitter
thread.*

3. Soak scarf in hot water using dye fixative for
20 minutes. This will keep the purples and
blues from making the yellows muddy. Place
scarf in washing machine with a bath towel (to
balance weight in machine and provide
friction) on delicate cycle in warm or cool
water. Use a mild detergent and small amount
of fabric softener. Place scarf in dryer with
towel on coolest temperature and gentlest dry
cycle. Remove from dryer, making certain scarf
is completely dry or it will wrinkle.

4. Refer to plied fringe diagram below. Cut
knots from unwoven warp and make plied
fringe by tightly twisting clockwise two groups
of three ends each. Put the groups together, let
them untwist counterclockwise, securing with
an overhand knot. Trim uneven ends.

special care:
Dry cleaning preferable. Scarf could be carefully
hand washed in cold water using mild
detergent. Rinse with fabric softener. Lay flat to
dry. Excess water may be blotted with a towel.
When scarf is almost dry, place in dryer with a
towel and dry on lowest heat for a few
minutes to fluff.

plied fringe diagram

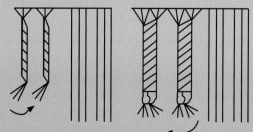

Paula Chafee Saardanalie

Paula Chaffee Scardamalia has an extensive educational and practical background in art and textiles. After receiving her B. A. in English & Creative Writing at Pennsylvania State University, Paula went on to study at the Smithsonian Institution in Washington, DC. She studied and assisted in quilting, counted-thread embroidery, and creative stitchery under the direction of Joan H. Koslan Schwartz. From there, Paula attended the Haystack Mountain School of Crafts at Deer Isle, Maine. Under Ferne Jacobs, she studied and assisted in loom and off-loom techniques. Later, again under Ferne Jacobs instruction at the International College, Los Angeles, California, she received her M. F. A. in Studio Arts.

Paula now maintains her own studio, Nettles and Green Threads, in Berne, New York. She states, "Weaving is an ancient technique rich in culture, tradition, magic, and beauty. Born from necessity thousands of years ago, it has evolved into an expression of story and color that carries an archetypal strength to the modern conscience."

Nettles and Green Threads was derived from a classic German fairytale steeped in sacrifice and determination, enchantment and love. It is a story of redemption and transformation. "For me," Paula says, "this is the essence of my work. Transformation - spiritual, physical, emotional . . . magic - through the weaving of intense color and luxurious texture. With a keen sense of connectiveness to the power of hue, pattern, and texture, I hope to transcend

the notion of designing fabric and rather, create pieces that tell a story, evoke a feeling. For me, this is the true art of weaving - an unconscious journey to clothe the soul and illuminate the spirit."

From September through December of 1996, Paula was invited to show her artwork and designs at five invitational exhibitions around the country. She exhibits her artwork and designs at several national trade shows, annually. Paula also has placed her line in a few select galleries and shops throughout the United States.

Paula has included additional photos of "gallery" scarves that demonstrate what can be accomplished after mastering this technique.

I learned how to hand-knit at an early age from my mother and a close family friend. I was an avid knitter of other people's patterns until a fellow artist suggested that since I would work into the wee hours of the night on a sweater and leave my paintings undone for months, I might want to put my own art ideas into my knits; thereby fulfilling my creative urges with my knitting obsession."

Rebekah Younger, creator of Younger Knits, shares a live/work loft space in Oakland, California, with her husband, Guy Marsden, an artist/engineer. She states: "Color, bold and bright or soft and subtle, excites me the most. Whenever I walk into a yarn shop, with hue upon hue lined up along the walls, I am always inspired to create.

I began designing art-to-wear as an outlet for this creativity. With a degree in Fine Arts from Beloit College in Wisconsin, designing my own garments is a way to incorporate my love of fiber with my art background.

Rebekah studied pattern writing and machine knitting at the Textile Arts Center in Chicago for two years and continued her training working independently for five years as a pattern writer/designer and sample maker for other Bay Area sweater manufacturers. She now markets her own line, Younger Knits, through high-quality crafts fairs, galleries, and clothing stores nationwide.

"My unique signature of blended color developed when I moved to California in 1988. I was drawn to the exquisite and ever-changing West Coast sunsets as a source of inspiration. I shot rolls and rolls of film, trying to capture the moment-to-moment changes in the sky."

Rebekah's pieces are featured as "gallery" scarves and demonstrate what can be accomplished after mastering this technique.

Rebekah Younger

The runway did not do **Robin Bergman's** line justice. Her pointillism-like knitting becomes even more fascinating when touched and seen up close. Her craftsmanship is raised to the level of couture in an area that defies the very category.

Her use of color and texture has become her hallmark.
  –Robert Rowe, Maverick Magazine, Fall 1993.

Since 1984, Robin Bergman, creator of Robin's Originals, has hand loomed limited edition and one-of-a-kind knitted artwear from luxury yarns and natural fibers drawing on her background as a painter (M.F.A. from Maryland Institute College of Art) and her experience as a textile conservator at the Isabella Stewart Gardner Museum in Boston, Massachusetts.

Loom knitting is a manual process like weaving using a knitting machine. "The making of knitted work is particularly challenging because the fabric, patterning, and shaped garment pieces are created simultaneously," Robin says. "My emphasis is on treating the sweater surface more like a canvas, experimenting with surface design and unusual juxtaposition of color, texture, and pattern—painting with yarns.

"Handmade garments are unique in the way that they transcend conventional boundaries. They can simultaneously be objects of art and of utility. They can also appeal to multiple senses, providing sophisticated visual and tactile pleasure even while offering simple warmth and comfort. Knitted fabrics, in particular, defy the usual boundaries of style. They can be comfortable and modern, yet elegant."

Robin's unique style has received accolades and awards from all areas of the arts and crafts industry, including several prestigious Niche awards.

Robin's pieces on pages 98–100 are featured as "gallery" scarves and demonstrate what can be accomplished after mastering this technique.

Scarf designed by Robin Bergman   Model Ryanne Webster

Scarf designed by Robin Bergman

ikat scarf

designed by Chapelle

materials:

fabric dye for cotton: desired color
yarn: 10/2 mercerized cotton, desired color
   for warp; 10/2 mercerized cotton, desired
   color (or white then dye) for weft

implements:

dowels: width of warp (2)
ikat tape or natural raffia
masking tape

instructions:

Refer to **general instructions** on pages 8–10.

weave: warp face weave.
finished dimension: weaver to determine width
   and length of scarf.
epi: 40
ppi: 16

1. Warp cotton at 40 epi. Tie cross securely but loosely enough for dye to penetrate.

2. Place dowel through each end of warp and stretch warp between two stationary points. Spread warp to desired scarf width. Tape to dowels. Using ikat tape, cut into 18" lengths, tear into approximately ⅜"-wide strips, and tie. If using raffia, cut into 24" lengths and tie. *Note: Raffia will not cover area as well as ikat tape.*

3. Ikat tape or raffia needs to be tied very tightly around warp strand to resist dye. See **diagram 1** on page 102.

4. Ikat pattern is created by tying off six ends ¾" long, see **diagram 2**, followed by 13 ends, see **diagram 3**, beginning where six ends left off for ¾", leaving 1½" between tying on the length. Allow 40 warps between tied off sections. See **diagram 4**. Repeat this process until all appropriate areas of warp have been tied.

5. Once all warp ends are tied off, the yarn is ready to be dyed.

6. Mix dye, following manufacturer's instructions. Leave yarn attached to dowels. Dip warp yarn into dye with dowels sitting on top of dye pot. Allow dye to reach desired

color. Remove yarn from dye pot and rinse until water runs clear. Remove warps from yarn. Hang warp up to dry.

7. When warp is dry, follow regular warping directions for loom using a warp faced weave.

special care:
Machine wash scarf, delicate cycle. Lay flat to dry. Comb out fringe.

ikat scarf diagrams

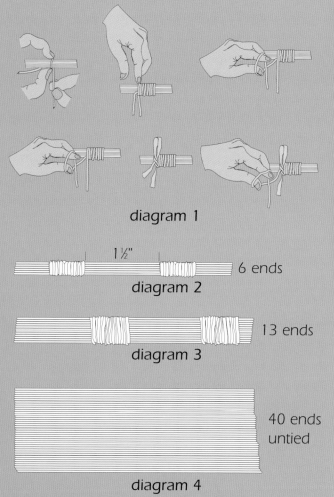

diagram 1

1½"

6 ends

diagram 2

13 ends

diagram 3

40 ends
untied

diagram 4

The pieces created by Joanna Chrysohoidis on pages 102–103 are featured as "gallery" scarves and demonstrate what can be accomplished after mastering this technique.

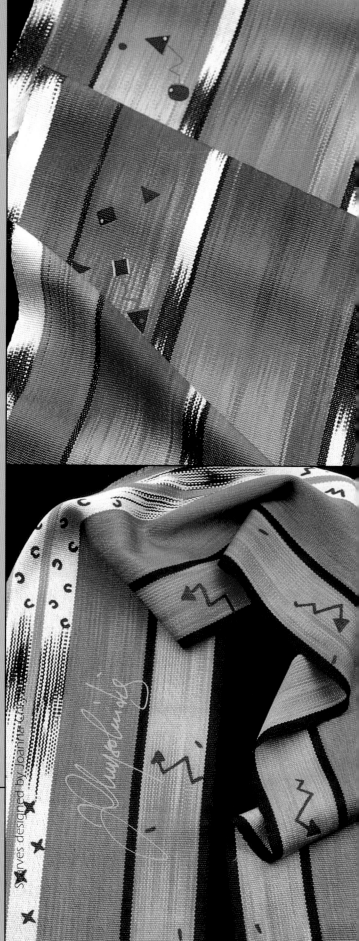

Scarves designed by Joanna Chrysohoidis

Born in New York in 1961, **Joanna Chrysohoidis** moved to Greece when she was eight years old. While there, she began working with surface designing at the age of fifteen, studying under Ann Citron in Athens for two years.

"Although a fifth-generation weaver," Joanna says, "I am essentially self-taught, having bought my first loom in 1982." She created her first weavings in 1983.

Joanna's designs appear in several publications and have received excellence awards in various shows. Her artwork and designs have been represented at industry exhibitions since 1991, and can be found in prestigious galleries and personal collections throughout the country.

"Watching my vision come to life," says Joanna, "first as a fabric, then as comfortably designed garments is what inspires me to create. Each piece is a one-of-a-kind, titled piece of art."

Currently residing in Asheville, North Carolina, **Pamela Whitlock**, creator of SOSUMI, began her career in weaving almost 30 years ago. Pamela was born in Pittsburgh, Pennsylvania, educated at Antioch College in Yellow Springs, Ohio, and has since attended the Penland School with Randall Darwall and Jason Pollen.

Over that period of time, she has experimented with a wide variety of weaving techniques. "I found my 'niche' some years ago," Pamela states, "concentrating on the complex system of shadow weaving."

By combining the wonderful tactile fibers of silk, rayon, and chenille with the visually exciting patterns of shadow weaving, Pamela is able to create a sumptuous fabric that is delightful to look at, sensuous to touch and wear, and maintains supple draping qualities.

Pamela's original SOSUMI line of scarves and shawls has expanded over the past few years to include garments, table linens, and home accessories. "I am pleased to offer as the newest addition to my SOSUMI designs, an on-going line of quilts featuring my hand-woven fabrics."

Pamela's piece is featured as a "gallery" scarf and demonstrates what can be accomplished after mastering this technique.

abbreviations:
K   knit
P   purl
st(s)   stitch(es)

instructions:
1. With blanc, cast on 37 sts. Work six rows seed st (K1, P1).

2. Using corresponding yarn colors and keeping four sts on each edge in seed st, work center 29 sts in stockinette st following **chart a** until piece measures 3" from beginning.

3. Work pattern following **chart b** over center 29 sts. Continue in stockinette st and **chart a** until piece measures 37" from beginning. Work pattern following **chart b** over center 29 sts. Continue stockinette st and **chart a** for 2½".

4. Work six rows seed st. Bind off. Make 6" fringe on each end.

chart a

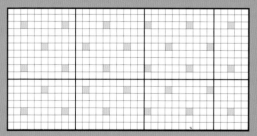

chart b

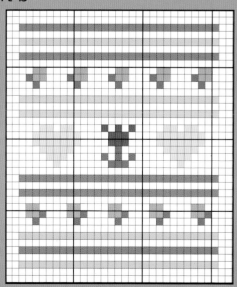

knitted hearts scarf
designed by Chapelle

materials:
Phildar pronostic: 2 balls #10 blanc; 1 each
   #36 flanelle, #49 lupin, #33 eucalyptus
Bucilla melody: 1 ball #34 tea rose
DMC pearl cotton (used double throughout):
   1 skein each #502 blue green, #932
   antique blue-lt., #522 violet-dk.

implements:
knitting needles: size 6
guage: 6 sts = 1"

Penny Toliver has spent most of her life raising her three children in Ogden, Utah. Now that her children have grown and set out on their own, Penny has redirected her energy to the art of knitting.

"I had to prove to my kids I can do something other than domestic in my life," Penny explains.

Penny learned to knit during a plane flight to Santa Fe, New Mexico. A friend brought her knitting material on the flight and showed Penny the basics of knitting. "I'm not very crafty," she admits, "I've done a little painting, but I got hooked on knitting."

After only a few years experience, she is now creating wearable art family and friends fight over.

Penny Toliver

knitted mittens & scarf

designed by Penny Toliver

materials:
yarn: double knitting chenille, 50g

implements:
needles: #6 U.S. 4½mm for scarf; #3 U.S.
  3¼mm; #4 U.S. 3½mm for mittens
crochet hook: size G, U.S.

abbreviations & symbols:

alt	alternate
beg	beginning
cont	continue
cn	cable needle
foll	follow
inc	increase
K	knit
K1	knit 1 stitch
P	purl
P1	purl 1 stitch
patt	pattern
psso	pass slipped stitch over knitted stitch
rem	remain(ing)
rep	repeat
rs	right side
SL1	slip one stitch knitways
slp	slip one stitch purlways
st(s)	stitch(es)
tog	together
ws	wrong side
yfwd	yarn forward
in	inches
cm	centimeters
mm	millimeters
*	Indicates that work following the * is to be repeated number of times * is indicated.
( )	Indicates that what is enclosed in the ( ) is to be repeated number of times indicated.

M1	Make a stitch by picking up horizontal loop lying before next stitch and working into the back of it.
Rib	1st row: *K1, P1, rep from * to last st K1. 2nd row: *P1, K1, rep from * to last st P1. rep 1st and 2nd rows.
Moss stitch:	Rows 1, 3, 5, and 7: knit. Rows 2 and 6: (ws) P1, *K1, P1 to end. Rows 4 and 8: (ws) K1, *P1, K1 to end. Rep rows 1-8.
T5R	Slip 3 st onto cn and hold at back of work, K2 then P1 from cn.
T3B	Slip 1 st onto cn and hold at back of work, K2 then P1 from cn.
T3F	Slip 2 st onto cn and hold at front of work, P1 then K2 from cn.
C3R	Slip 2 st onto cn and hold at front of work, K1 then K2 from cn.
C3L	Slip 1 st onto cn and hold at back of work, K2 then K1 from cn.
C6	Slip 3 st onto cn and hold at back of work, K3 then K3 from cn.

scarf instructions:
Refer to **general instructions** on pages 8–10.

To knit cabled scarf use #6 U.S. needles. Cast on 67 sts. Work in moss st for eight rows.

Proceed as follows:
<u>Row 1:</u> (K1, P1) twice, P1, K6, P1, K43, P1, K6, P1, (P1, K1) twice.

Row 2: (K1, P1) twice, K1, P6, K1, P43, K1, P6, K1, (P1, K1) twice.
Row 3: (K1, P1) twice, P1, KC6, P1, K43, P1, KC6, P1, (P1, K1) twice.

Rep row 2 once.

Rep rows 1 and 2 three times.

Row 11: (K1, P1) twice, P1, C6, P1, K19, T5R, K19, P1, C6, P1, (P1, K1) twice.
Row 12: (K1, P1) twice, K1, P6, K1, P21, K1, P21, K1, (P1, K1) twice.
Row 13: (K1, P1) twice, P1, K6, P1, K18, T3B, K1, T3F, K18, P1, K6, P1, (P1, K1) twice.
Row 14: (K1, P1) twice, K1, P6, K1, P20, K1, P1, K1, P29, K1, P6, K1, (P1, K1) twice.
Row 15: P20, (K1, P1) twice, P1, K6, P1, K17, T3B, K1, P1, K1, T3F, K17, P1, K6, P1, (P1, K1) twice.
Row 16: (K1, P1) twice, K1, P6, K1, P19 (K1, P1) twice, K1 P19, K1, P6, K1, (P1, K1) twice.
Row 17: (K1, P1) twice, P1, K6, P1, K16, T3B, (K1, P1) twice, K1, T3F, K16, P1, K6, P1, (P1, K1) twice.
Row 18: (K1, P1) twice, K1, P6, K1, P18, (K1, P1) three times, K1, P18, K1, P6, K1, (P1, K1) twice.
Row 19: (K1, P1) twice, P1, C6, P1, K15, T3B, (K1, P1) three times, K1, T3F, K15, P1, C6, P1, (P1, K1) twice.
Row 20: (K1, P1) twice, K1, P6, K1, P17, (K1, P1) four times, K1, P17, K1, P6, K1, (P1, K1) twice.
Row 21: (K1, P1) twice, P1, K6, P1, K14, T3B, (K1, P1) four times, T3F, K14, P1, K6, P1, (P1, K1) twice.
Row 22: (K1, P1) twice, K1, P6, K1, P16, (K1, P1) five times, K1, P16, K1, P6, K1, (P1, K1) twice.
Row 23: (K1, P1) twice, P1, K6, P1, K14, C3R, (P1, K1) four times, P1, C3L, K14, P1, K6, P1, (P1, K1) twice.
Row 24: rep row 20.

Row 25: (K1, P1) twice, P1, K6, P1, K15, C3R, (P1, K1) three times, P1, C3L, K15, P1, K6, P1, (P1, K1) twice.
Row 26: rep row 18.
Row 27: (K1, P1) twice, P1, C6, P1, K16, C3R, (P1, K1) twice, P1, C3L, K16, P1, C6, P1, (P1, K1) twice.
Row 28: rep row 16.
Row 29: (K1, P1) twice, P1, K6, P1, K17, C3R, P1, K1, P1, C3L, K17, P1, K6, P1, (P1, K1) twice.
Row 30: (K1, P1) twice, K1, P6, K1, P20, K1, P1, K1, P20, K1, P6, K1, (P1, K1) twice.
Row 31: (K1, P1) twice, P1, K6, P1, K18, C3R, P1, C3L, K18, P1, K6, P1, (P1, K1) twice.
Row 32: (K1, P1) twice, K1, P6, K1, P21, K1, P21, K1, P6, K1, (P1, K1) twice.
Row 33: (K1, P1) twice, P1, K6, P1, K19, T5R, K19, P1, K6, P1, (P1, K1) twice.
Row 34: (K1, P1) twice, K1, P6, K1, P43, K1, P6, K1, (P1, K1) twice.

Rep rows 3 to 34. Work to desired length, 48" to 58", ending row 34.

Rep rows 3 to 8 once. With rs work eight rows in moss st. Cast off in patt.

To complete, use four strands of yarn 13" long on ws, insert crochet hook from front to back through piece and over folded yarn. Pull yarn through, draw ends through and tighten.

mittens instructions:
To knit cabled mittens use #3 U.S. needles. Cast on 43 sts.

Left hand:
Row 1: (rs) rib, K1, *P1, K1.
Rep from * to end.

Row 2: rib, P1, *K1, P1.
Rep from * to end.

Rep rows 1 and 2 for 2" ending with a 1st rib row.

Inc row: rib to end, inc 1st at end of row 44 sts.

Change to #4 U.S. needles and work 6 rows in stockinette st (1 row K, 1 row P) starting with a K row. ***

Next row: K19, M1, K2, M1, K to end.
Next row: P to end.
Next row: K19, M1, K4, M1,K to end.

Cont to M1 at each side of thumb gusset as before on 2nd and every foll alt row to 54 sts, ending with P row.

Work two rows.
Shape thumb.

Next row: K32, cast on 1st turn.
Next row: P14, cast on 1st turn.
Working on these 15 sts only, work 12 rows.
** Shape top.
Next row: (K2 tog) seven times, K1.
Next row: P to end.
Next row: (K2 tog) four times, K1.
Run yarn through rem sts. Draw up and fasten off. **

With rs of work facing, rejoin yarn to rem sts, pick up and K2 sts from base of thumb, K to end (43 st) **.

Next row: P to end.
** Work 24 rows.

Shape top.

Row 1: K2 tog, K18, SL1, K2 tog, psso, K to last 2 sts, K2 tog.
Row 2 and every foll alt row: P to end.

Row 3: K2 tog, K16, SL1, K2 tog, psso, K to last 2 sts, K2 tog.
Row 5: K2 tog, K14, SL1, K2 tog, psso, K to last 2 sts, K2 tog.
Row 7: K2 tog, K12, SL1, K2 tog, psso, K to last 2 sts, K2 tog.
Row 9: K2 tog, K10, SL1, K2 tog, psso, K to last 2 sts, K2 tog.
Row 10: P to end, 23 sts.
Cast off.**

Right hand:
Work as given for left hand to ***.

Next row: K22, M1, K4, M1, K to end.
Next row: P to end.
Next row: K22, M1, K4, M1, K to end.

Cont to M1 at each side of thumb gusset as before on 2nd and every foll alt row to 54 sts, ending with a ws row.

Work two rows.
Shape thumb.

Next row: K35, cast on 1st turn.
Next row: P14, cast on 1st turn.
Working on these 15 st only, complete as given for thumb of left hand. With rs of work facing, rejoin yarn to rem st. Pick up and K2 sts from base of thumb, K to end 43 sts.
Next row: P to end.
** Work 24 rows.

Shape top same as left hand. Make up. Sew up all seams.

special care:
Hand wash scarf and mittens in cold or warm water. Lay flat to dry.

tying & wearing scarves

Photographed by
Ralph Gabriner
Model Tracy Coogan

Photographed by
Ralph Gabriner
Model Violetta Klimczewska

Photographed by
Ralph Gabriner
Model Violetta Klimczewska

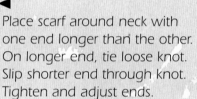

Place scarf around neck with one end longer than the other. On longer end, tie loose knot. Slip shorter end through knot. Tighten and adjust ends.

Loosely tie single knot at center of scarf. Place at front of neck with ends to back. Cross ends and bring to front. Pull ends through knot and adjust.

Spread scarf out with wrong side up. Lift fabric at center and knot. Flip scarf to make triangle with knot inside. Take opposite corners and tie loosely at back of neck.

(1)

(2)

(3)

(4)

1. Make an overhand knot.

2. Make a bend in standing part.

3. Tie working end around bend forming second knot.

4. Be certain loops are equal.

Bows can be tied & worn around the head, neck, or waist.

Place package in center of square. Fold two opposite corners in. Fold and crease other two corners up. Tie knot.

Place package in center of square. Fold bottom one-third up. Fold left one-third over. Fold right one-third over. Fold remaining two corners in and tuck into flap.

Place ball
in square.

Fold two
opposite
corners up.
Tie other
two corners
at back,
then front.

Tie top of two
remaining
corners
together.

Knot one corner,
Push other corner
through.

115

Fold two bandanas or
square scarves in half.

Knot center together.

Tie top ends together.
Roll bottom two ends.
Tie at the back.

Place long scarf over top of head. Twist over at back.

Bring to front and twist over again.

Tuck in ends.

▲

Place center of oblong or folded scarf at crown of head. Cross ends under chin and bring to back. Cross ends in back and return to front. Tie loosely or let ends hang.

▼

118

▲ Start with oversized shawl. Wrap around waist so ends overlap. Cinch waist with belt or tuck into waistline.

Fold oversized square into large triangle. Place point of triangle in front, crossing ends in back. Bring ends forward, twist slightly and tie double knot in center of triangle. ▼

▲ Place center of scarf at front of neck with ends to back. Cross ends, bring to front. Flip one end over the other.

119

Wrap oblong scarf around neck. Cross ends twice at front. Bring ends back, tie off, and adjust.

Loop right end of scarf over left. Take left end around and over right.

Bring left end through newly formed bends.

Tighten knot evenly.

The front looks like a square.

The back looks like a cross.

Twist oblong scarf into a tight wrap until it coils on its own when ends are brought together. Double scarf and wrap around neck. Bring ends through loop formed at center and adjust.

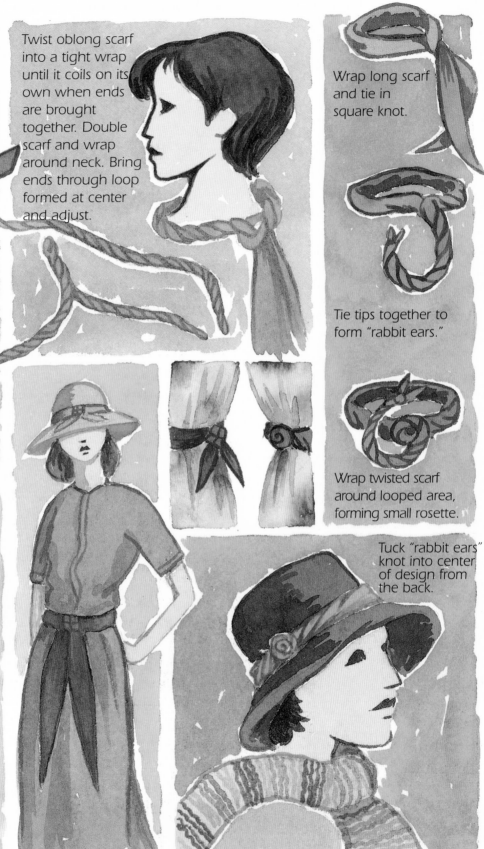

Wrap long scarf and tie in square knot.

Tie tips together to form "rabbit ears."

Wrap twisted scarf around looped area, forming small rosette.

Tuck "rabbit ears" knot into center of design from the back.

decorating with scarves

opposite: A natural arrangement for a favorite scarf is found in draping it over the end of a bed or accenting a trunk top or chair back.

above: Scarves add a special touch when displayed in unexpected places—try wrapping one around a garden statue, that has been brought in for the winter months, or spilling out of a vase stuffed with silk flowers.

Scarf designed by Cynthia Elmore

above: It is said that one picture is worth a thousand words and it is never more true when the "picture" is one that you have created. A perfect example is a hand-made scarf displayed in the home as a decorating accent. It tells family and friends a lot about you and what you love!

above: Beautiful hand-made scarves should never be stored out of sight in a closet or a drawer. Showcase them for all to enjoy on an antique hat rack or an ornate victorian towel hanger.

above: Tablecloths can transform a room simply and inexpensively. Scarves are even more versatile and affordable than purchased table linens. Try using a series of small scarves rather than the expected single large table cloth.

metric equivalency chart

mm-millimetres   cm-centimetres
inches to millimetres and centimetres

inches	mm	cm	inches	cm	inches	cm
⅛	3	0.3	9	22.9	30	76.2
¼	6	0.6	10	25.4	31	78.7
½	13	1.3	12	30.5	33	83.8
⅝	16	1.6	13	33.0	34	86.4
¾	19	1.9	14	35.6	35	88.9
⅞	22	2.2	15	38.1	36	91.4
1	25	2.5	16	40.6	37	94.0
1¼	32	3.2	17	43.2	38	96.5
1½	38	3.8	18	45.7	39	99.1
1¾	44	4.4	19	48.3	40	101.6
2	51	5.1	20	50.8	41	104.1
2½	64	6.4	21	53.3	42	106.7
3	76	7.6	22	55.9	43	109.2
3½	89	8.9	23	58.4	44	111.8
4	102	10.2	24	61.0	45	114.3
4½	114	11.4	25	63.5	46	116.8
5	127	12.7	26	66.0	47	119.4
6	152	15.2	27	68.6	48	121.9
7	178	17.8	28	71.1	49	124.5
8	203	20.3	29	73.7	50	127.0

yards to metres

yards	metres	yards	metres	yards	metres	yards	metres	yards	metres
⅛	0.11	2⅛	1.94	4⅛	3.77	6⅛	5.60	8⅛	7.43
¼	0.23	2¼	2.06	4¼	3.89	6¼	5.72	8¼	7.54
⅜	0.34	2⅜	2.17	4⅜	4.00	6⅜	5.83	8⅜	7.66
½	0.46	2½	2.29	4½	4.11	6½	5.94	8½	7.77
⅝	0.57	2⅝	2.40	4⅝	4.23	6⅝	6.06	8⅝	7.89
¾	0.69	2¾	2.51	4¾	4.34	6¾	6.17	8¾	8.00
⅞	0.80	2⅞	2.63	4⅞	4.46	6⅞	6.29	8⅞	8.12
1	0.91	3	2.74	5	4.57	7	6.40	9	8.23
1⅛	1.03	3⅛	2.86	5⅛	4.69	7⅛	6.52	9⅛	8.34
1¼	1.14	3¼	2.97	5¼	4.80	7¼	6.63	9¼	8.46
1⅜	1.26	3⅜	3.09	5⅜	4.91	7⅜	6.74	9⅜	8.57
1½	1.37	3½	3.20	5½	5.03	7½	6.86	9½	8.69
1⅝	1.49	3⅝	3.31	5⅝	5.14	7⅝	6.97	9⅝	8.80
1¾	1.60	3¾	3.43	5¾	5.26	7¾	7.09	9¾	8.92
1⅞	1.71	3⅞	3.54	5⅞	5.37	7⅞	7.20	9⅞	9.03
2	1.83	4	3.66	6	5.49	8	7.32	10	9.14

index